Go Ahead and Laugh

A Serious **Guide to Speaking** with Humor.

Go Ahead and Laugh:
A Serious Guide to Speaking with Humor.
Copyright ©2009, 2011 Rich Hopkins

"Stop!" and "Chapter One Author's Preface" ©2009 Dan Weedin
"Who's Gonna Know?" and "Chapter Two Author's Preface" ©2009 Palmo Carpino
"The River of No Return" and "Chapter Three Author's Preface" ©2009 Sarfaraz Nazir
"The Big V" and "Chapter Four Author's Preface" ©2009 Russ Dantu
"Beware of Ladies' Night Out" and "Chapter Five Author's Preface" ©2009 Kay Fittes
"Getting the Message" and "Chapter Six Author's Preface" ©2009 Charlie Wilson
"Laughing in Everyday Life" and "Chapter Seven Author's Preface" ©2009 Carrie Warren
"Rules to Live by When Calling 911" and "Chapter Eight Author's Preface ©2009 Terry Canfield
"Hey! Watch This!" and "Chapter Nine Author's Preface" ©2009 Douglas Wilson
"KIDS" and "Chapter Ten Author's Preface" ©2009 Susan Lamb
"Question Man" and "Chapter Eleven Author's Preface" ©2009 Michael Davis

All rights reserved. No part of this book may be reproduced or transmitted in any form or by any means, electronic or mechanical, including photocopying, recording, or by any information storage and retrieval system, without permission in writing from the publisher. Brief quotations embodied in critical essay, article, or review is allowed. These articles and/or reviews must state the correct title and author(s) of this book by name.

2nd Edition Published by Perflexativity Press
247 Cypress Lane
Broomfield, CO 80020

Published in the United States of America and Canada
Edit, Layout, and Cover Design: Perflexativity Press

'Go Ahead and Laugh' is a great resource for anyone looking to add humor to their presentations. By including entire speech texts and then analyzing those speeches, the book creates a simple but powerful structure that moves beyond theory and into application.

- Avish Parashar, Speaker, Humorist, Trainer
www.MotivationalSmartAss.com

What do you get when you gather a mixed bunch of speakers and humorists, blend with some behind the scenes insights, and analyze their presentations? Go ahead and laugh, but you get a seriously funny resource for adding or enhancing the humor in your presentations.

- Bob 'Idea Man' Hooey, Accredited Speaker
Canadian Association of Professional Speakers
(Charter Member)
www.IdeaMan.net

This book totally rocks! It teaches you how to take your boring presentations and make them funny - I wish I would have had this book when I was starting out!

- Andy Dooley, Professional Speaker, Law of Attraction Artist,
Spiritual Comedian
www.AndyDooley.com

Insightful and Funny...
As a student of comedy and humor, Rich Hopkins' 'Go Ahead and Laugh' is truly a blueprint for any person wanting to add humor to their speeches. The pragmatic yet easily implementable approaches on how to get people to laugh is what makes this book very unique and worth studying.

-Johnny "The Transition Man" Campbell
DTM, Accredited Speaker
Author of '21st Century Speaker'
www.21stCenturySpeaker.com

What a unique approach to understanding humor in speaking! You "meet" the author, glimpse behind their pen and into their thoughts - read the set-up, indulge in their speech - then an analysis of the humor techniques and delivery mechanics - with tips how to use them!

This book teaches how to use humor as the medium for the message, especially when the message may be one of sensitivity or potentially controversial. The insightful teaching aside, each speech in this book is a sparkling gem!

- Sheryl Roush, President, Sparkle Presentations, Inc.
Accredited Speaker, Trainer, Speaking Coach
www.SparklePresentations.com

This is a unique creation, a case study approach to humor in speaking - eleven great speeches, each one analyzed to teach the reader valuable lessons about the hard work of making people laugh. A valuable resource for any speaker!

- Colin William
2008 World Champion of Public Speaking Finalist

Acknowledgements

There are so many people to thank for bringing this book to fruition including:

Kristi, my patient and long-suffering bride.
My six children, who bring me laughter daily.
My co-authors, who have stood by me from day one.
My friend Terry Canfield, who has blessed my family.
My hero Darren LaCroix, who went to extraordinary lengths to help me out when chips were down.

Thank you to these and others who stood by me when laughter seemed furthest from reality.

We're done!

Go ahead and laugh!

Table of Contents

Page 8   About the Author

Page 10   Introduction

Page 11   An Interview with Darren LaCroix

Page 23   The Speeches

Page 24   Dan Weedin   Stop!

Page 37   Palmo Carpino   Who's Gonna Know

Page 46   Sarfaraz Nazir   The River of No Return

Page 57   Russ Dantu   The Big V

Page 67   Kay Fittes   Beware of Ladies' Night Out

Page 77   Charlie Wilson   Getting the Message

Page 87   Carrie Warren   Laughing in Everyday Life

Page 103   Terry Canfield   Rules to Live By When Calling 911

Page 113   Douglas Wilson   "Hey, Watch This!"

Page 128   Susan Lamb   KIDS

Page 140   Michael Davis   Question Man

Page 150   Punchlines

Page 153   Resources

Rich Hopkins

A student of communications on stage, from the platform, as well as the sales and marketing arena for over twenty years, Rich Hopkins works with professionals from all walks of life, transforming them into effective, efficient and energizing speakers.

Rich leverages his extensive field experiences to create specialized communication strategies, boosting his clients confidence and honing their messages to create positive business results.

At the age of 13, Rich faced his first audience — a classroom of hostile fellow 7th graders — as he presented a report on President Abraham Lincoln. Rich only made it through one paragraph before fear and embarrassment sent him running out the door in tears. The next year, determined to prove to himself he could speak in front of others, he took a drama class, which allowed him to shine for the first time on the stage.

Rich appeared in several stage plays in college, from Oliver to Harvey to the Importance of Being Earnest, and applied his well-honed acting skills in the real world of marketing and sales after graduation. In 1999, Rich joined Toastmasters, where he no longer had the crutch of great playwrights to lean on — he was forced to find messages of his own to share with his fellow club members. Before long, he found himself placing in the Top 20 speakers out of 200,000 Toastmasters worldwide, and has appeared in the World Championship of Public Speaking in both 2006 and 2008, placing as high as 3rd in the world.

Rich is known for bringing out the true personalities of his clients, refusing to create speaking clones of himself. Instead, his tailored approach leads each individual to find their own stories, leverage their own experiences, and give themselves permission to speak with authority in their careers and personal lives.

"I truly enjoy watching people find themselves, and give themselves permission to share who they really are with the world," Rich says. "When the lightbulb goes on, and they realize that who they are and what they have to say truly matters, it is an amazing sight to witness."

Rich Hopkins is one of today's premier speaking coaches whose clients quickly realize their speaking abilities are about to undergo for a once-in-a-lifetime transformation — as they begin to share themselves with the world.

In addition to coaching speakers, Rich speaks to audiences as "The Champion of Choice", using his own experiences to illustrate how we create our lives through our choices each day. His daily blog, at ChampionofChoice.blogspot.com, features daily video entries as he discusses his own daily choices, from failures and frustrations to successes and celebrations.

Contact Rich Hopkins to inquire about Speaking or Coaching at Rich@RichHopkins.net

Sign up for your weekly motivational/speaking skills newsletter at www.RichHopkins.com, and grab your copy of his free e-book The Finalists: 2008 - a behind the scenes look at the World Championship of Public Speaking from the point of view of all 10 contestants!

Introduction

As if public speaking weren't hard enough, now I'm expected to be funny?

When was the last time you listened to a boring speaker? Why were they boring? Content? Tone of voice? Complete disconnection from their audience?

When was the last time YOU were the boring speaker?
It's not your fault. Really. We've been brought up to believe two things about public speaking that are taken as absolute fact:

1. *People fear speaking in public more than death*, and
2. *You can't learn to be funny*

Neither are true. Tell someone to give a speech or you'll shoot them, and they'll give a speech, 99% of the time. As for being funny? By the end of this book you'll learn at least 33 humor techniques to guarantee you never bore your audience again.

The book you hold in your hands features a mixture of speeches, showcasing both corporate comedy and humor for entertainment's sake. You will meet the author, and get an understanding of who is behind the material, as well as an in-depth look at why and how they created their speech. You will have the script of their speech, often with stage direction and additional comments – much like a director's copy of a movie script. Finally, I will provide an analysis of humor techniques used in each speech, and suggest how those techniques may be adapted to your purposes.

After all, in today's world of speaking, you are, indeed, expected to be funny. To use humor to connect, to lead your audience in learning through laughter, and to keep your listeners on their toes, waiting for their next chance to titter, giggle, and snort. Go on - Go Ahead and Laugh!

An Interview with
Darren LaCroix

When many of us imagine comedy, our minds take us to stand-up comedy, with names crossing the generations from George Burns to Bill Engvall, Richard Pryor to Joan Rivers, George Carlin to Jeff Foxworthy, and dozens more. The quick-witted, hard-hitting humor seems beyond our imaginations – how could we, ordinary citizens of the planet, ever be as funny as Bill Cosby, Rodney Dangerfield, or Jerry Seinfeld?

Speaking with humor, however, isn't stand-up comedy. To get the inside scoop on the differences, I thought I'd give stand-up comedian, keynote speaker, and 2001 World Champion of Public Speaking Darren LaCroix a call, and ask. **(Below is a transcript of our conversation).**

Why did you choose to become a comedian?

It wasn't a decision to become a comedian. Many of you know the story, but I used to own a Subway sandwich shop, and literally things were so bad I had to go back and get a day job in order to pay my own employees!

I was kind of at the lowest point in my life, and a buddy of mine gave me a motivational tape, and on the tape, Brian Tracy, he asked a question. He asked "What would you dare to dream if you knew you could not fail?" And I thought "I'd be a comedian!" That'd be the ultimate. I mean, to make an audience laugh and earn a living at that, that would be the ultimate.

And then all the sudden this little doubting voice said "But that's not you Darren, you're not funny!" But that wasn't the question. The question wasn't "What do the High School Aptitude Tests say you should pursue?", it was "What would you dare to dream if you knew you would not fail?"

So it was really that question that was the catalyst, but then, I thought "Y'know, if I'm gonna try this, I'm really not funny, I really want to give it my all." So I told my friends and my family that I wanted to try this and they kinda laughed at me (ironically), I just didn't get any support that I should try it – no encouragement. But I started thinking about it and its human nature to think "Oh here's a guy who's not funny, he shouldn't be a comedian". That kind of logic. However, **people who are successful think differently than everybody else.**

So I thought if I'm going to be a comedian, I should probably ask a COMEDIAN! On a Friday night I went to a little comedy club in Worcester, Massachusetts, a gentlemen walked up me, Chris McGuire, (he's still a writer in Los Angeles, super guy) and he suggested two things:

#1 - goto open mic night and watch other people who are just starting out, because you need to compare yourself to other people who are brand new. You want to learn and be inspired by people who ARE the best, but you only want to compare yourself to other people who are new. Don't compare yourself to the experts.

#2 – go get *Stand-Up Comedy: The Book* by Judy Carter (a book I highly recommend). I went and got the book and did the exercises. A lot of people will go buy a book but they won't actually read it, or if they do read it, they won't actually do the exercises. But I really, really, *really* wanted to give this my all, and quite frankly, I thought "I'm going to give this my all, and then after I fail, I'm never going to do this again" But I didn't want to regret later in life, thinking I attempted it, but only half-heartedly. So it was April 26th, 1992, **Stitches**, in Boston, I went up for the first time. It was horrible - in fact I just made one mistake that I just kind of reacted myself to "Aw Shoot!" (that's not really what I said, I actually said the swear word), but then all the sudden everybody LAUGHED! I'm looking around in shock and I'm thinking that's not where you're *supposed* to laugh, but I'll take it!

That was the only laugh I got that night. But it didn't matter, I was bit by the bug and I wanted more. I thought "Even though it was a mistake, I still got the end result that I was looking for" So if that's the case then maybe I can reproduce that. If I had five minutes of things that don't work and one thing that did, all I have to do is get rid of the things that don't work, and reproduce the thing that did. I've been doing stand-up comedy ever since that night.

What's the difference between being a stand-up comic, a humorist, and a speaker who uses humor?

To a comedian, humor IS the message. Meaning, after a comedian does their routine (if they're really good), people leave with less stress because they've laughed, and they leave thinking he or she was funny. A humorist, or a speaker that uses humor, uses humor as the medium for the message. That's really the biggest distinction between the two.

Why does humor work in more serious speeches?

What humor does is get us to want to listen. Unless we truly have the audiences attention, and truly have them listening, I don't think our message is heard. It's so difficult in this day and age to gain the audiences full attention, to have their rapt attention. Since media is so strong and prevalent in our lives we see thousands and thousands of messages. We see with TV that Hollywood uses so much money to keep our attention that we've almost become accustomed to being spoonfed. So if you can be funny, it increases attention, which gets you hired more, which gets you paid more, because it's what people want [to hear].

We want to learn, but we want to laugh. When I'm doing a paid keynote speech I'll always ask the meeting planner "What percentage humor vs. what percentage message are you looking for?". I want to know if they're looking for more of a purely entertaining speech (90/10), or looking for 50/50, but I've got to know what they want to be able to deliver that. So its always an important question, and they usually have to sit there and think about it for a minute, because they know clearly in their mind, but until I understand what they want, I really don't know exactly how to approach it.

Are there any speeches we might give where humor might not be appropriate?

I think humor is always appropriate...99 percent of the time! One of the most difficult speeches is when somebody passes. Usually, because the humor is a release of tension [its appropriate]. Where the most tension lies, it gives us the most potential for humor. That's why at a funeral or a wedding you'll see people laughing going into crying going into laughing again because they are both closely related emotions. They're both releases of tension. Even the most tragic situations – we need that release. We want that release, just so we can deal and cope. Its a coping mechanism.

Now there may be one or two times where humor is not appropriate. I don't think the time when you're laying off half the company is a time to use humor. I believe there are circumstances for most people when it just wouldn't be appropriate. If people are laying off or you are announcing that someone passed away. Steve Allen said it best: "Comedy equals tragedy plus time", but we need that time to elapse in order to make the humor appropriate. We want to have that humor, but not just yet. We want to feel the pain, we need to go through the emotions first.

For example, when September 11th happened, Letterman and Leno both stopped doing their opening monologues. They still had their shows, but they started right behind their desks, and started with interviews. It was about two weeks into it, I remember David Letterman sitting behind a desk and just testing jokes, FROM BEHIND THE DESK. It's kind of a test. I think we all need to remember that even the greatest comedians are testing. The humor went over so well because we were dying for that laugh, we were dying for that release. We had gone through some of the grieving and now we needed that help.

Where are the best places to use humor in your speech?

Strategically through the speech. I think it varies from speaker to speaker, message to message, but bottom line is it should be *uncovered*, as Craig Valentine (World Champion of Public Speaking, 1999) would say, you want to uncover the laughter, you don't want to add humor. Adding humor is like putting a Band-Aid on a bad speech. It could be a funny joke but chances are it came from somewhere else, or it takes us off-track of the message in the story, so even though it might be funny, its not congruent with the message and where we're going. I think the bottom line is the more humor the better, but then you have some speakers that are purely entertaining, and the message is lost. What's your reason for being there [to speak]?

[Darren goes on to discuss humor enhances our messages:]

To paraphrase Jeffrey Gitomer: At the height of laughter is the height of listening. That's really where we want to spoonfeed our message in, after the big laugh. Now we're open...now we gotta slide that message right into our brain...now its time. Because if you have another big laugh coming after that, now its going to dilute the message. It's going to take over the message and be more powerful. You want the big message to come after the laughs. In the comedy world I was always taught after you get the biggest laugh, thats' when you walk off stage, you want to leave 'em laughing. In speaking, you want to leave them thinking – big difference.

A great example of humor in a painful situation is my comedy mentor Dave Fitzgerald who was diagnosed with cancer years ago. He had an amazing attitude. He looked at things in a very funny way, but he was very scared like everyone else who was diagnosed with cancer. He was petrified, but he used [humor] as his coping mechanism, to help him and his family and friends to cope with his situation.

He was one of the first comedians ever, in the late 90s, to use the word cancer on stage. It was unheard of then, it was the black word that you never said on stage, but he found a way to make it work. I think if your message is important, if you care about it enough, if you're passionate about it enough, you'll see it through to figure it out. I'll always remember watching him experiment on stage, and I'd pull him aside offstage and say "Dave what are you doing, this is crazy, its not working." he said "Darren, I care too much about my message to not try and figure it out. I need to figure it out and I will find a way."

He did find a way, he found an incredible way to make it funny, and he realized the audience was so caught up in what he was saying that he had to cushion it first, and let them know he was doing ok, and he had fully recovered. Once he finally put that disclaimer in there, he talked about the situation where he was diagnosed with bladder cancer, and they actually told him they had to remove his bladder. Dave, with his incredible attitude and in his infinite wisdom – the doctor asked him what kind of bladder would he like? He said "I'm thinkin', BIGGER! I want a three-movie bladder! I want to watch the whole Godfather trilogy". That being said, they actually created a bladder out of pieces of his intestine, which, through the miracles of modern medicine, that's amazing! He said "Great! Darren, I was excited! But if you look at it from the intestines point of view, its not a promotion. One day you're in food service, the next day you're in waste management!"

It was a powerful message, but it was used with humor. You're talking about cancer. Dave said "Darren, what we're talking about is not making fun of the disease, but we're making light of the human side of it". Because he was the patient, it was acceptable for him to talk about it. You wouldn't want to be talking about someone else who had cancer, unless it was a close friend, and it was in endearment.

Is there ever a time a 'street joke', or internet joke, is going to work in a speech?

Depends on the event. If you're at a funeral, you would tell it there, then its appropriate [based on audience expectation]. Other than that, if you're a professional, an emerging professional should never ever use a joke you found on the internet, even though some people do and get away with it, doesn't mean its fine. As soon as we hear something we've heard before, (you know the funniest jokes have been around the internet a thousand times, thats why they're funny and that's why you found out about them) [we know it].

If you're truly a professional, you should be telling your stories, your perspective, that's why we give you the privilege of our time to listen. I don't ever think it's ever appropriate for someone who's a professional. I'll admit, early on in my comedy career, there were lines that I heard that I thought it was okau to use. There are, in the comedy world, some stock lines for handling hecklers, that's different. Those are accepted to use. But if you're using some other material that you heard from some other speaker, its plagiarism. We all know the best speaker's material. Now we question your credibility and your ethics. It's not worth the risk if you're serious about this business. Humor is serious business.

How do we find humorous stories?

Some people say "Oh, its so hard to find stories!" WHAT? Are you crazy? Are you on Crack? There are stories all around you! Walk through an airport *once,* you should have twenty stories of things you see and observations you have. You go through security once, you should have three stories right there. There's so many stories around, but here's the problem: we're not designed to look for things and categorize them as stories. They're all around us.

Ask yourself, when did you laugh today? Whenever you laugh you should ask yourself "Ooh, could that be a story?" Watching and looking and observing something that cracks you up. That should be the indicator – hey! Ding ding ding ding! This could be a funny story. Now what we need to do is figure out the point of the story and how we can use it and how we may embellish the story a little. When do you laugh during the day? The things that make you laugh are the stories you should be telling.

As Patricia Fripp, my coach says, the stories that you tell around the dinner table with your friends and family, those are the stories you should be telling from the stage. Call up your family and ask your siblings about when you were growing up. Ask them about what silly things you did or fought about growing up, *or anything*, and you'll have more stories than you need. Problem is, we see something, we laugh, and we see the story in the raw form, but then we see the speaker on stage give an amazing and hysterical story and we think "Wow, nothing like that happens to me." Well guess what, it didn't happen exactly that way, it had to be crafted into a story that worked. You don't see the diamonds in the rough. Every time you laugh, that should be a diamond in the rough and the potential of a story that can be massaged and rewritten into a great story.

Is sexual, political, or racial humor ever appropriate?

Who's your audience? Who's in front of you? If your speaking to a group of clergy, can you not talk about religion? You probably *need* to. You're talking at a nudist convention, or a nymphomaniac convention, you're not going to talk about sex? Absolutely you would. Its part of your audience and their lifestyle. I think there are appropriate times, but I think it matters who's the audience.

When I'm in front of a group of salesman, that may be 99% male, my job is to get my message to the audience. They're not going to like the cutesy jokes. With them, I have to get a little bit more in their face. I will go a little bit closer to that line. We need to understand as speakers where that line is. Most audiences, for people who are Toastmasters, that's a generic audience – but that's not the real world. The real world, there are [real] people out there...now I'm not saying you should talk about sex, I'm not saying you should talk about politics, and there's a way to talk about every subject without going over the line or getting too controversial. It depends on your audience, it depends on your message. You have to look at the big picture, look at why you're there and what you're trying to accomplish. Should it just be a joke for the sake of getting a laugh? Never. Never, Never, Never.

Does self-effacing humor hurt our credibility?

Quite honestly, if you're perfect, we don't want to hear from you. I think self-effacing humor is a great way to start, but I think you must consider the credibility of your audience. For example you may want to talk about how you used to do things, before you were enlightened in one of your expertises. You're making fun of you, but you're making fun of the old you, the younger you, the naïve you. Absolutely, that's appropriate.

I think self-effacing humor is a powerful thing. Of course, if you're a rocket scientist, you don't want to talk about the silo you blew up last week! I think common logic prevails, common sense prevails, but unfortunately in this world there's not enough common sense. I think its a good thing, I always will use self-effacing humor. We do need to be concerned about our credibility, but we shouldn't be the hero all the time. We can't put ourselves on the pedestal, [or] our audience won't relate to us.

I just went and spoke in Abu Dhabi, and my luggage never made it in, so neither did my suit. I'm smart enough to know that it happens, and it happened before. I don't worry about it. I'm there for my audience, I'm there for my message, and I don't like traveling for 30 hours wearing a suit – its just not going to happen. Because my luggage didn't arrive, I had to speak in jeans. I had a legitimate reason why, I told the audience right up front, I said "I apologize, I respect you guys immensely, but my luggage didn't make it in and my suits in my luggage. But my first message to you is, it's not about what I'm wearing, it's about where my heart is and what my audience leaves with."

I actually have a video of a gentlemen who came up to me after and said he was glad I was speaking in my 'casuals'. I did have jeans on, they weren't *that* casual, but he said "Sometimes, suits separate us." It was a powerful point and a powerful message. What he said was true, he could relate to me more because he saw me as an average person with a great process, rather than some 'ego-driven World Champion'. Its a great message for me, and you just have to be in the moment and go with the flow.

What do you do when your audience doesn't laugh, or laughs when they are not supposed to?

You need to always be 'in the moment'. If you're in the moment, you're ready for anything. I think every speaker should take an improv class. I think if we could all improvise better, and we could handle anything that comes at us, we'd be so much better as a speaker. It helped me immensely. In my World Championship speech I had laughs that never came in my practice, and I'd practiced it 22 times! You can almost see the expression on my face of surprise when they're laughing. I'm like, "hey, what are you laughing at? Nobody did that in rehearsal!

When I speak in Asia, in other cultures, they don't laugh on the lines that are ALWAYS funny in the U.S. or Canada, and they laugh in places I don't even know what the heck they're laughing at. I have to be so comfortable with me and what I'm doing and what I'm trying to accomplish, and let go of these little surprises and have fun with it. Y'know, if they start laughing, go with it! Shut up – stop moving your lips, and let 'em laugh! Doesn't matter how it happened. Go back and check out the recording to try to figure it out if you can. Ask someone after for insight into the culture. Why was a specific line funny? I don't know, I don't have to know, and we'll never know it all.

We have to be comfortable with getting responses that we didn't expect, whether it be good, whether it be bad. I can't get upset at an audience because they didn't get something that I was trying to communicate that always works. I might have been a little off that day. I might not have realized that in their culture this means that, or such and such. There's always going to be that, especially when there's traveling internationally. There's a big difference in humor, absolutely a big difference.

I was asked once to teach humor in Malaysia to a group of Toastmasters, and I thought "Hey, if that's what you want, that's what I'll do," but I realized it was one of my biggest bombs ever, because the humor is so different in different cultures, it was a mistake to try and teach it – they don't think the way we think. So even though some parts might work, I'd never done that before, so I would've had to do more research in that area to figure out how or why. We live and we learn and we move on, and I survived that. Now I know. I get asked to teach humor in the Middle East and I just said no – I don't think that's the best use of my time, there's so much more I know I can teach, and I know will work.

We as speakers are going to have to know that we're going to have surprises. Here's the beauty of the surprise: you get the laugh you didn't expect, or you don't get the laugh you did expect, it means there is a learning point there. So anyone who's serious about speaking should be recording themselves. If you're really serious, we should be going back, saying "Why did they laugh? Why didn't they laugh? What was different?" If you can start figuring those things out, you'll figure out the key to your own persona, and your own speeches, and your own humor. But if you just let it go, you've missed a learning point.

What should our readers do after finishing this book?

I think every speaker should take an improv class, and if they want to add humor, consider taking a stand-up comedy class near them. It's a different animal. Understand that just because you've been a speaker for years, you go do stand-up and you are in a whole 'nuther world. You are not in Kansas anymore. That experience, if you're open to it, will help you to grow everywhere. I take improv classes, I still take acting classes, I still learn everywhere I can. We should never be done, especially if you want to learn humor.

Final Words

You want to be funnier? I have one bit of advice: Stage Time, Stage Time Stage Time. Record it – then go back and learn from you own personal successes and your non-laughs. Check out *Stand Up Comedy: The Book* by Judy Carter. You can also find the 4 CD set called *Learn How the Pros Make 'em Laugh* at my website, www.DarrenLaCroix.com. I also teach humor at HumorBootcamp.com with my comedy mentor here in Las Vegas. When you check in at the website, be sure to look for my free newsletter - as well as many more valuable resources.

Darren LaCroix

2001 World Champion of Public Speaking

Stage Time
Stage Time
Stage Time!

The Speeches
Go Ahead and Laugh.

Dan Weedin

Looking for a corporate trainer that will get the results you need, leave your staff in stitches, and have them coming back for more?

Do you have an upcoming event and the keynote speaker needs to hit a home run with your audience?

Dan is an award-winning speaker that provides practical insight and know-how of someone who has been there and done that. Dan engages his audience by using humor, charisma and compassion.

Outside of work, Dan is actively involved with Rotary, Toastmasters, and youth sports. He has been married to his high school sweetheart for over 20 years and is the father of two teenage daughters and his loyal dog Charlie. He is an avid golfer and enjoys being "The Voice" for the local high school football team, serving as their stadium announcer since 2004.

"He challenged our employees to apply new concepts in different ways and to tailor them to our specific industry. The workshop was organized, educational, and motivational. Most importantly, Dan kept it fun and our employees felt very much a part of the process."
- **Kyle Kincaid, Vice-President Parker Lumber Co, Inc. (Bremerton, WA)**

Contact him today and start getting the results you deserve.

Toro Consulting
www.DanWeedin.com, Weedin360.com (blog)
DanWeedin.tv (YouTube), @danweedin (twitter)
Email: info@danweedin.com
Phone: 360.271.1592, P.O. Box 1571, Paulsbo, WA 98370

Author's Preface

Have you ever stumbled on to a great idea? If so, you will understand how my 2007 International Speech Contest speech for the District level was born. It was ready to go a full two months in advance. There was no doubt about it. Nothing could change my mind. Yeah, right! *Famous last words.*

I was given the opportunity to give a 'regular' speech at my Toastmasters club in late February. I didn't want to give the speech I'd planned on competing with so as not to introduce it to my future audience. I figured I'd just give a fun, light-hearted speech on a story I loved to tell. In going through my story file, I found just the right one.

Teaching my oldest daughter Mindy to drive was a real family event. Recently licensed, she was chomping at the bit to get started. I was much less enthusiastic. That Sunday after church, my wife Barb said, "This would be a good time to have Mindy drive. The weather's perfect; the parking lot is empty; We have to start sometime". "OK", I thought. After all, we had just gone to church. We at least had THAT going for us!

The experience was just about how the story you will read actually went, so I won't blow it for you. That being said, there wasn't much humor or laughter at the time. If you're like me, you've found is that this is a perfect recipe for a future humorous story.

After I had calmed down and Mindy progressed as a driver, I found myself regaling that Sunday afternoon drive at family gatherings. Everyone laughed, even Mindy. I even used it as a 'horror" story to all my friends who had kids coming up to driving age. What fun!

I realized that this would be just the humorous story I could use to give to my club. Little did I know at that time it was the beginning of a great ride.

The speech was originally titled *"Life in the Fast Lane"*. It was a big hit at the club. I even won best speaker for the evening. When I got home, I thought that maybe I could use that in the Fall Humorous Speech Contest.

Have you ever felt something was just wrong...OR just right?

I started practicing my contest speech and something was just wrong. My mind kept drifting back to my speech about Mindy. I kept telling Barb, "You know. I really like that speech. In fact, I think I like it better than the contest speech". To that, my sharp wife keenly asked, "Then why don't you use it for the contest?" Good question...

My response was that it didn't have an inspirational message. So I kept on working on the other one. I even sent it to 1999 World Champion Craig Valentine to critique. That became the moment that *"STOP!"* became truly born.

Craig wrote back with a critique on my contest speech. It wasn't terrible, but it also wasn't pretty. I could see that my "sure-fire" winner wasn't quite ready for the dance. It was at that moment that my wife's voice echoed in my head...

"Why don't you use it for the contest?"

At that moment, I tossed the other aside and began working in earnest on *"Life in the Fast Lane"*.

I'm a huge believer in the concept of mentoring. I finally saw the correlation of teaching a kid how to drive with teaching them how to live life. I figured this was a good metaphor and would be the carry-out message.

That being said, it was also a good time to practice what I preached so I called on some mentoring help for myself. As a member of an organization called Champions Edge, I had access to former World Champion Speakers to receive feedback on my speeches. I sent the speech again to the Champions Edge for a critique. This time, I got 2001 Champ Darren LaCroix. This would be a defining moment.

Darren gave me some valuable feedback and I massaged the speech to give to my club on April 10, 2007. I won the contest and was feeling very good about myself and *"Life in the Fast Lane"*. That following weekend, I attended a boot camp with Darren and Craig in Dallas. I was going to hire Darren to help me move on the competition trail, even though I thought it was a bullet-proof speech. Yeah, right! Famous last words.

Darren gave me some excellent advice in making the speech more humorous. Primarily, it came in my timing.

- I made the opening more drawn out by delivering a pained, anxious opening that built the level of curiosity in the audience. I then hit them with the punchline which every adult parent could identify with. Even if you just remembered learning how to drive, you had a vivid image.

- He showed me how to use the "Rule of Three "strategy more effectively in both writing and delivery. The third word was the diversion that was to be funny – I learned how to properly deliver that for best effect.

- I learned that I needed to give the audience time to laugh. This was more than simply avoiding stepping on your laugh (talking before the audience is done laughing). It also meant pausing long enough for them to "get it" and laugh.

All this timing meant that I needed to work that into my concern for time. Because time is a huge factor in contests, I needed to pare away at other lines that weren't as important. The consequence was a more tightly written speech that made more sense to the audience.

One last thing Darren advised was to change the title of the speech to "*STOP!*" It was a quick, fun, and accurate title. It gave me the opportunity to use the word stop as part of a humorous and impactful set of lines in the speech.

Recently, I was invited to speak at the Toastmasters Region 1 Humorous Speech Showcase in Seattle. If you know me, you won't be surprised that I jumped at the opportunity. You may have been surprised to know that I took my inspirational speech "STOP!" and decided to turn it into a strictly humorous speech. Why?

I knew that this was a very funny story that related well with everyone. Some of the biggest laughs I ever received were from this speech. I decided to take out the "message" of the inspirational speech and make it all funny. So I added a third story at the end. The new story really didn't happen at the same time as the first. It had come weeks later during another trip. That didn't matter for the story. All that mattered was that it built on the humorous "conflict" of the original. In the end, it worked better than I had anticipated. I had many people who were familiar with my original speech who liked it even better as a humorous speech. Go figure!

The bottom line is this: In order to create a funny story that will work well and draw laughs with any audience, you need to remember the following things…

1. Find personal stories that you love to tell to family and friends. They may not have been funny at the time, but most of the funniest things you've seen are borne out of "tragedy". Think about it. Your favorite situational comedy on TV is full of "tragedy" for the protagonist, but you still laugh. The same is true in your life.

2. Don't force humor. As Craig Valentine says, you must "uncover" humor. You "uncover" it by finding what makes others laugh in your stories.

3. Use good timing techniques. Pauses are everything in comedy. Have you ever watched Jack Benny? You must anticipate the laughter and be prepared to pause.

4. Don't step on your laughs. You may not even expect your audience to laugh, but they might.

5. Be flexible. Don't fall in love with your speech to the point that you're unwilling to make changes that will benefit your story. You wouldn't believe how many tweaks I make on my speeches, including this one.

One final BONUS thought. Be open to the idea of mentoring. It doesn't matter how extensive your training is, there is always someone there who you can learn from. I know the most successful people are also the ones who continually strive to learn. Mentoring is a key part of my business philosophy. Consider it for yours.

I hope you've found value in my story and that you enjoy reading my speech. Humor is one of the great equalizers in life. It connects people along all lines of economic, cultural, and diverse backgrounds. Make it a part of your presentations and watch it impact your audiences. Have fun and keep them laughing;-]

Dan Weedin
June, 2008

Stop! *by Dan Weedin*

Mindy…easy, easy, wow,Wow, WOW, STOP!!!!!!
(hand to head – move to stool)

Madame Toastmaster, Friends, and anyone who's ever had to teach their kids how to drive…

Have you ever mentored a child? *(pause)* Who mentored you? *(huge pause)* A parent; a coach; a favorite teacher? Why do you think you still remember them?

Mentoring a child isn't always easy, but it's always worth the effort…

EVEN for us driving instructors; That little bundle of joy that you brought into the world 15 years ago, is now in control of a 6,000 pound wrecking machine; and your life, in a vacant parking lot…and you don't get a brake pedal on your side…and believe me, I tried using it! *(pretend to use brake pedal)*

(Leave stool)

Imagine a PEACEFUL Sunday afternoon. My newly permitted daughter Mindy needed to get some drive time, so my wife Barb and I decided it was time to take her for her maiden voyage. We were ready to boldly go where many parents have gone before...

Our destination - the high school parking lot. The perfect spot – no cars, no stop lights, no pedestrians.*No lawsuits!* As Barb was getting tightly strapped in the back seat with my younger daughter Kelli, who was grounded...*we thought this might scare her straight*... Mindy and I traded chairs; and as she was ready to go, I confidently proclaimed, like *Star Trek's* Captain Picard - "Make it so, Number One!".

With that, we went from zero to 60 *(pause)* feet *(pause)* in 33 seconds. Mario Andretti, she wasn't. More like Molasses Mindy!

I said, "Mindy...you can speed it up just a bit."
"DAD...stop yelling at me!"
"I'm not yelling...yet."
From the back Barb, said "She's doing just fine." *(roll eyes)*

We finally got Mindy moving in a straight line right down the middle of the parking lot at a blazing 5mph. "Oh yeah"...Life in the fast lane *(facetiously)*.

However, as we took a right to come back the other way...a terrible thing happened. She discovered the gas pedal. Like a magnet, we're headed straight for the embankment off the edge of the parking lot! *(move on stage)*

"Mindy easy, easy, wow,Wow, WOW, STOP!!!!!!

(Peek over the edge) Have you ever been this close to the edge? *(pause)* At this point I knew that in order to be truly effective as a driving instructor, you need patience, perseverance, and valium.

We backed her out and not long after she started getting the hang of it, a brilliant idea popped into my head. *(tap head)* Let's go out into the real world.

We weren't in the real world very long before I started thinking "Whose stupid idea was this anyway"? That's when…a terrible thing happened; I felt myself leaning to my right *(lean)*. All of a sudden, I saw a row of mailboxes approaching me faster than a galactic meteor! I screamed, "TURN" and we narrowly averted disaster! *(big gestures)*

Mindy screamed *(pause)* "Stop yelling at me!" *(hands shaking in the air)*

I screamed, "Grab the wheel!"

From the back, Barb said - "Mindy, pull over". I was thinking "She's going to get it now!"

But instead of acknowledging that I just saved the Starship Enterprise, I mean the car, Barb pointed at ME and said – "You" *(finger pointing)*, "in the back seat." *(show reaction)* I slinked to the back with Kelli - guess I was grounded, too** - and covered my face with my hat as we drove back to the parking lot.

Barb turned and asked me, "Dan, are you covering your face because you feel ashamed" I said "No dear…I'm covering my face because I'm terrified!" *(fearful reaction)*

Well, in spite of me, Mindy became an excellent driver and I became a better instructor. In fact, we recently took a trip to Seattle where she drove and I had my hat over my face again *(move to sit on stool)* this time because I was peacefully sleeping. *(pretend sleeping with head back)*

You know…teaching your kid to drive is an awful lot like teaching them how to make their way in the world…in the beginning there will be many false starts, violent turns, and close calls.

(Leave stool and move towards audience) You may even encounter a few precipitous cliffs. As a father of two teenage girls, I call those boys.

BUT...

If you think your time and teaching doesn't matter...STOP!

It does...

If you're thinking "my efforts don't make a difference"...Stop!

They will...

If you think they will reject you and you're teaching...YOU'RE RIGHT...they might... BUT don't let that stop you from making a difference.

Who taught you how to drive? Maybe it's the same person who taught you your greatest life lessons. How will you pass it on?

(Step forward)

GO!!! *(Arms extended to the audience)*

Analysis

Could you see and hear Dan deliver his first line?

"Mindy *(with trepidation in his voice)*...easy *(soft and slow)*, easy *(slightly louder and faster)*, Wow *(clear and strong, with urgency)*, WOW, STOP *(loudest, in combined fear, confusion and excitement)*!"

We've heard this tone before, used on us or used BY us. It's funny because: A. As a speaker, he sells it in his voice and facial expressions, and B. He's going through it, not us!

"*Stop!*" is an effective speech which offers the following methods you can duplicate as you speak.

> **1. Exaggerating the Familiar – Teaching Teens to Drive**
> The speaker paints a wonderful picture for us, bringing us a slice of his family life that has a broad baseline for all of us. Most of us have been on one side or the other of this scenario, or will be.
>
> **2. Using Self as Punchline –The Tense, Slightly Goofy Dad**
> The speaker positions himself as the fall guy. By encouraging us to laugh AT him even as we laugh WITH him, he builds a strong audience connection, preparing them to laugh, and eventually to accept a closing, inspirational point.
>
> **3. Dialog as Storyteller**
> It becomes about characters, drawing the audience into the scene. By opening with dialog, we immediately come into the scene. Contrasting dialog content and delivery, much can be said in few words. We hear the conflict without a long explanation being necessary to understand. Back and forth between father, mother, and daughter creates a triangle of perspectives that create humorous conflict.

4. Props
The stool becomes the vehicle, becoming a character in itself. By turning the stool consistently into the car (or starship!), the audience is instantly ready for 'vehicular humor' from that position on the stage.

5. Rule of Three – With and Without a Topper
With a humorous twist - 'Patience, perseverance, and valium' 'No cars, no stoplights, no pedestrians – NO LAWSUITS!' In these instances, the humor comes not just in the cadence, but by the payoff being an unsaid thought – creating humor that is covert and overt at the same time.

6. Catchy Cultural References
From its introduction with "boldly go where many parents have gone before' – the *Star Trek* reference was our cue that it was okay to take this part of the speech somewhat lightly, while creating an interesting image for us to call back as he followed up with 'Make it so" and "Saving the Enterprise".

7. Position Switch – Adult Becomes Child
By trading positions from teacher to bystander, going from 'savior' to 'grounded', the speaker becomes a sympathetic figure, and one open to learning a lesson for us, which he is then in position to pass on to his audience without bearing the 'authority' tag as much as an 'experience' tag.

At the close of the speech, the speaker makes his point: that the time we take to teach really matters. After entertaining us for 5/6th of the speech, he gives us a call back to reality. The audience is ready for something with substance after a steady diet of humor, and the quick twist to seriousness gives the final point impact.

Consider this approach when delivering a serious message that may be quickly dismissed on its own. Using humor to win over the audience, a speaker builds credibility quickly, and is able to transfer credibility to the ultimate point of the speech.

Palmo Carpino

Palmo is a talented humorist, presenter and coach. A DTM (Distinguished Toastmaster), member of Bedstone Olympics Toastmasters; Charter Member, Sponsor, Mentor and President of Wit Pleasure, Calgary's first Advanced Toastmasters club specializing in the development of humour in speech and presentation skills.

Starting off with a small improv group in the early 1980's, Palmo has entertained audiences with stand-up comedy at Yuk Yuks, The Sidetrack Cafe, Punchlines, The Comedy House, and several open mic performances including Las Vegas and New York. He is a popular Master of Ceremonies at special events including teachers' dinners, corporate lunch-and-learns, award banquets and receptions. He has been known to "speak for food." His name has appeared on the front cover of Canadian Geographic, TV Guide and Maclean's magazines on multiple occasions. (just on the mailing label but technically, still on the front cover). Palmo lives in Calgary with his wife Lorraine and their three sons Matthew, Giancarlo and Emilio.

When not embarrassing his kids in public or paying for therapy, he is a Production Artist for the marketing and communication strategy firm Applied Communications.

For more information, or to contact Palmo Carpino, visit him at www.palmocarpino.com or email him at carpinop@telus.net

Author's Preface

February 7, 2004, Calgary, Alberta – The Omnipotent Story-Telling Idol competition (TOSTI's) was an initiative spearheaded by the Calgary bureau of VoicePrint with co-operation from the Calgary area Toastmasters, representatives from Dale Carnegie, the Canadian Association of Professional Speakers (CAPS) and other organizations with an interest in storytelling, broadcasting and public speaking. The event featured numerous storytellers, a dinner and over three hours of entertainment. After the opening comments and introductions, the stage was set for the ten storytellers to share their tales about the contest theme: "The history books were wrong…"

When I was initially writing my story, I knew I would be in competition with a much wider group of contestants than those in the Toastmasters realm. I knew I had to bring my 'A-Game' – vocal variety, gestures and probably a prop. I wrestled with the idea of props because, up to this point, the majority of my speeches relied most heavily on timing, wit and very specific phrasing.

Wordsmithing, I feel, is usually the best goal. With props there is a greater chance of relying far too much on the visual and not on, what I have always thought to be, the imagery painted by carefully crafted wording and sentence structure.

However, I finally resigned myself to the fact that I would lean more toward the visual for two reasons: first, the audience would not be completely filled with Toastmasters who would perhaps be thinking the same way I was. I put myself in the seats of others and surmised I would be more entertained and visually captivated if I was taking in more than just the spoken word. Although I had not finalized exactly what it was I would be highlighting, I knew it would need to be "big." The room would be holding almost 200 people and would be more deep than wide. The stage was only slightly raised.

The second reason I would be going more visual was the simple fact that the audience would see (and hopefully recognize) the character, and they could simply listen to the story in the manner it was intended. But no. I couldn't nail the accent so I had to go with the bigger visual.

I strut onto the stage with slicked-back hair, a Bible under one arm and present my entire speech wearing nothing but a fig leaf and lots of gold chains. A big fig leaf. In fact, my initial premise for this speech was based on one single solitary movement. The leaf, which is oval in shape with a definitive pointed end, starts off in what would be considered a horizontal placement at my waist. When I make my way to center stage there is usually a good ten to fifteen seconds of laughter, cheers and jeers. Before I even say my first word, and while the audience is slowing down to a respectable dull roar, I take the leaf, rotate it 90 degrees so that the sharper end which was originally pointing to the right (as viewed by the audience) is now pointing straight down (less area covered from side to side and now more area covered from top to bottom). This brings on another wave of five to ten seconds of laughter. Eye contact with one or two audience members right up front is crucial. It's acknowledged with a finger point, a wink and an 'I know you want me' attitude which is directed to one person but seen by the entire crowd.

Intrigued? Read on...

Who's Gonna Know? *by Palmo Carpino*

(Enter stage right)

(Adamo, jet black, slicked-back hair; multiple gold chains adorn his neck and chest; a Bible is carried in left hand approximately mid-chest level; the only clothing is leaf-covered shorts positioned at waist level, struts to center spot)

(Large leaf adjustment)

How you doin'? I'm here to tell ya the history books was wrong. My name is Adamo – it comes from 'Adam,' meaning first guy and 'O,' meaning from Italy. Now, this particular book here *(show Bible)* is not so much wrong as much as it is misinterpreted. In the beginning there was nuttin'. I mean absolutely not a thing – not even darkness. God, having a little time on his hands, decides to start something. He was also pretty smart. I guess you could say he was the very first 'wise gawd'. With stuff he just happens to have lying around – some cosmic dust, some protons, neutrons, ping pongs – buddabing buddaboom! I've got your big bang theory right here.

Once things starts to cool off he starts his organization - not The Organization but rather starts organizing the things he's created *(opens book and appears to be reading/skimming)*. He starts separating the sky from the earth; the land from the sea; the night from the day *(right arm wide sweeping as though a conductor in front of an orchestra).*

While creating the animals he gets interrupted. Seems like there is this udder guy who thinks he's boss, trying to muscle in on God's turf, see? Here's where I comes in. He creates me so I can help him out. Mainly, to name the animals.

"Adamo," he says, "I need a favour." How can I refuse? This is the almighty wise gawd; The Cappo de Cappi; the Big Boss.

I says no problem. So I starts namin' my friends the animals – Frankie the Ferret, Dominic the Rat; Tony the Mole; Johnny the Weasel; Enzo the Polecat. I have no idea what's a polecat?! God returns a little while later. Looks around and is pretty happy wit' me and I quote, "And God saw that it was good."

"Adamo, this pleases me. Now what can I do for you?" I says fugeddaboudit. I do for you, maybe someday you do for me...? *(sly shrug)*

"No, this deserves some compensation. Anything. You just name it."

I'm thinkin', well, I could maybe use someone to cook a lil' somethin' for me. I do have some leaves to be cleaned and ironed. And it does get a lil' lonely at times, the nights get a lil' cold – we ain't exactly on the equator here if you get my drift.

"I will create for you a mate and she will be spectacular. She will do for you what needs to be done – cook your food, clean your clothes and keep you warm at nights."

Whoa, this sounds too good to be true. What's the catch? What's it gonna cost me?

"A woman like this doesn't come cheap. A woman like this might cost you an arm and a leg."

Hmmm. Whatcha got for a rib?

Then *(reads from the book again)* God causes the man to fall into a deep sleep *(looks back up to the audience)* by creatin' a couch and a remote control. Now I have no idea how long I was out for but when I wakes up I see a beautiful creature in front of me. And a big scar on my chest – it sort of matches the one on my face. Honestly, she wasn't much of a looker but I liked the way she was dressed...what could I say? Nothin'. That's what she was wearin' – nothin'.

God tells us, before you two love boids get to know each other, *(read from book)* "Remember this one thing – you may eat of any of the fruit in the garden except for..." Blah blah blah...I didn't exactly hear the whole thing. I did hear something about, "For if you do, surely you will die." So that's her name...Shirley.

"And much sorrow will enter into the world if you do – pain and suffering, rising interest rates, death, taxes and in-laws. Don't blow it."

We've got the garden to ourselves – we're frolicking because that's what you do in gardens. I got no idea how much times goes by cuz we are just frolicking our brains out. Even this gets a little tiring after a while so I needs to take a nap. Where's my remote?

While I take a nap, she takes a walk and meets up with a snake. He says to her, "Did God really say you shouldn't eat of this tree for surely you shall die?" She looks around a couple of times. Who's Shirley?

Even though she hadn't been around for any great length of time she knows enough that this can't be good. How do you trust a guy with no kneecaps? Or knees? Or legs?

She starts to back away and bumps into a vine, you see – a grape vine. Grape, from the Italian 'grape-ah,' meaning elixir of the gods, and 'vine,' meaning you can floss your teeth with this thing! The grapes, they fall to the ground. She stomps on them. Now she's really panicking. Running to the couch she comes and wakes me and asks me what I think we should do. I says, what do you mean we?

Alright, alright. No problem. All we gotta do is get rid of the evidence. We start stuffin' them into our mouths. Hey, not half bad and the evidence is gone. We accidentally bump off a few more of the grapes and get rid of more of the evidence. Funny thing, the more evidence we get rid of, the better she starts to look.

She looks at me, laughing at, I dunno what, and says, "Do you think we are gonna get in trouble?"

I says to her *(pulling an apple out from my shorts)*, "Ah, fugeddaboudit *(take a bite out of the apple)*. Who's gonna know...?"

(exit stage right)

Analysis

Editor's note: Palmo didn't know we were going to analyze his speech, so he provided his own analysis. I found it to be spot-on, and include it below, with additional comments to close.

Stage Persona (and/or accents)
I start off with the (stereo)typical 'How you doin?' in my, mediocre at best, New York Italian accent and go straight into my, "Da history books wuz wrong," intro – the theme for that year's competition. Phrasing and pronunciation of certain words reiterate the style of character narrating the speech. Could this speech have been presented sans the persona, completely straight and fully dressed? Sure. Would it have received the same amount of laughter and made the same connection with the audience? Probably not.

Innuendos
The speech is riddled with subtle, and not so subtle, mob-like innuendos from gangster slang and repeated gestures (see below). The beauty with not spoon-feeding the audience with every fine detail, as is also illustrated in pauses, is that you allow them to conjure up hilarious images and conclusions that surpass what could've been provided.

Gestures
The majority of gestures such as strutting on stage in the beginning (pun intended), head tilts, apparent nervous twitches and anxious sideway glances are directly related to the character that is being portrayed. Others, such as the conductor-like movement of the arms during the creation, simply add to connecting with the audience – especially when you have a room that is deeper than it is wide. You need to hold on to the people in the cheap seats way in the back.

The Recognized
The fact that the audience would be familiar with the story and/or characters helps in establishing a connection. When using a well-known punchline (the cost of such a mate…what you got for a rib?), it needs to be delivered in such a way that the audience doesn't know what hit them until either after the fact or at the last possible moment. This is what gets you, at the very least, an, "Okay, you got me," kind of chuckle – instead of that telegraphed, "I've heard it before," groan.

Callbacks
An example of this is illustrated in the repeated use of the word 'surely', as quoted from scripture references, and also portrays (I believe) a double-entendre since it is used as the female name Shirley. Traditionally, a callback would be used the second or third time in different circumstances, not exactly the same as in this presentation.

Props
The use of props within a speech is always of concern – a double-edge sword of sorts. If it adds to or complements your message it can draw your audience in that much more. If it is distracting to the point where they are focusing on the item instead of on your words, lose the prop.

The use of the Bible is substantiated because of the multiple instances where the character is reading direct quotes and scriptural reference. The Apple, although seen only during the final few seconds of the speech, is a well-known item in regards to the story.

It is strategically brought into the speech at the end so that no one will be concerned about what happens to a half-eaten piece of fruit if introduced at any other part of the presentation. Also, never talk with your mouth full. Costume, or the lack there of, is referenced in the Preface.

Postscript
As an aside, the participant who ended up finishing third - and who did an excellent job for her age - was a young girl representing at a speaking club at the Calgary chapter of the (CNIB) Canadian National Institute for the Blind. That's right, I was up against a 13 year-old blind girl (in pigtails). Are you kidding me? Why didn't you put her in a wheelchair and stick a puppy in her lap while you were at it! -- Sheesh!

Editor's wrap-up: If you're a beginning speaker, you are probably shaking your head, wondering how you could ever pull off a speech as you've just read it! While the speaker benefits from experience and confidence, he carries into the speech a key that is accessible to any speaker at anytime. That key is background research. He looked closely at what his audience would accept from his speech, and went in knowing that his methods would be accepted and appreciated.

As you face speaking opportunities, investigate your audience. Will they accept humor packaged as it is in *"Who's Gonna Know?"*?

By knowing ahead of time what their boundaries are, you prepare yourself to stay within them, and identify where stretching them will both create humor and accomplish the goal of your speech.

As well as knowing the audience, know YOURSELF. Don't deliver material that makes YOU uncomfortable. The audience will pick up on it immediately, and either wonder why you think its acceptable for them if it isn't for you, or resent being used as a barometer for your boundaries. While it is essential to stretch your speaking skills, do it in front of a supportive crowd, instead of a pay-off audience.

Sarfaraz Nazir

Born in Shadiwal, Gujrat, in the north central Punjab region of Pakistan, Sarfaraz was raised in Karachi by the Arabian Sea (Indian Ocean). He learned about working hard and putting family first from his father, Commander Nazir of the Pakistan Navy.

Sarfaraz learned about giving selflessly from his mother, Begum Nazir. Even though she only completed a few years of school, she strongly believed in the value of education. All of her children are educated; they include an engineer, a medical doctor, a bank officer, a textile manufacturing plant owner, a graphic artist, and a teacher.

During high school, Sarfaraz wrote articles for one of Karachi's major English newspapers, *The Morning News*, and also for the second-leading Urdu newspaper. He participated in school speech and debate contests. In addition to competing in track and field competition, he played cricket, field hockey, and soccer.

Sarfaraz left his home, as a teenager, to attend Oklahoma State University in Stillwater. He received an MBA degree in Management and an undergraduate degree in Industrial Engineering.

Sarfaraz's major business accomplishments include the design, development, and delivery of a Leadership Development Program for front-line managers and supervisors for the nation's largest consumer electronics manufacturer. He implemented an Honor Payroll System for production workers called the No-Punch Bunch System for the telecommunications division of a major oil company. He helped implement a Unit Cost Tracking System for the world's largest aircraft manufacturer.

Sarfaraz joined Toastmasters International in 1993, and received his DTM designation in 1997. He was a presenter in the Speakers Showcase at the Toastmasters International Annual Convention in San Diego in 1995. Sarfaraz has taken second place twice — representing District 25 in 2000 and District 50 in 2007 — in the Region III International Speech contests. Since 1996, he has competed nine times at the district level in the International Speech contest; taking first place three times, second place three times, and third place twice. At the region level, he's competed against Ed Tate, 2000 World Champion of Public Speaking, and Jim Key, 2003 World Champion of Public Speaking. In 2008, he competed at the District level against eventual World Champion of Public Speaking LaShunda Rundles.

Sarfaraz was named District 25 Toastmaster of the Year for 1997-98. He received the Professional Excellence Award from the American Society for Training & Development in 1995. He was named the Analyst of the Year by the Society of Cost Estimating and Analysis in 1985. He received the region-level Distinguished Service Award from the American Institute of Industrial Engineers in 1986.

Sarfaraz's mission and purpose in live is to live life to the fullest. His focus in life is faith, family, friends, financial freedom, and fun. He believes in giving the gift of money, the gift of time, and the gift of love. He is passionate about the Toastmasters program. He has mentored several Toastmasters, and has sponsored several new clubs.

Sarfaraz's presentations and seminars include "The Power of WoW: How to Design, Develop, and Deliver a Winning Presentation," "If Only I Had a Dream — Living with Purpose, Passion, and Persistence," and "I-Behave: Understanding Styles."

Sarfaraz resides with Linda, his wife, a former high school teacher, in Arlington, Texas. Their three children, Nafisa, Shahzad, and Shazia, also reside in the Dallas-Fort Worth metroplex.

Sarfaraz Nazir
Alternate Contestant
World Championship of Public Speaking, 2007 & 2000
SNlistens@yahoo.com
www.SNPresentations.com
PO Box 180241
Arlington, TX 76096-0241
(817) 233-6076

Author's Preface

After winning the District 50 International Speech contest in 2007, I had six weeks to prepare a new speech; some might say that this was quite a luxury. I knew that I wanted the speech to be MY story -- an emotional story with a strong message. I also knew that no one was going to get sick or die in my speech; you can find plenty of that on the ten o'clock news. I selected a personal story that included my family, both in Pakistan and in the United States. The story was ninety seconds long. My challenge was to stretch it into a seven-minute speech and present it with aplomb. As time passed by, I had no earthly idea what I wanted to do.

David Hostler, Past District Governor, knew that I was raised by the ocean and that I had a passion for water, waterfalls, and the power of water. He sent me an e-mail saying, "how about something with water, the sea, ….?" The lights came on. The water metaphor. One week after winning the district contest, I had an idea for a new speech – my life's journey in light of the water's journey. It took two weeks to prepare the first draft. It took me another three weeks to practice at several clubs and to fine-tune the speech. I am grateful to many Toastmasters in Districts 50 and 25, as well as 1990 World Champion of Public Speaking (WCPS) David Brooks, Darren LaCroix (2001 WCPS), and Mark Brown (1995 WCPS), for their feedback, help, and encouragement.

I wanted to ensure that humor was sprinkled throughout the speech. David Brooks says that a speech should have the right mix of message and humor. I wanted to put the audience on an emotional roller coaster. I recalled Ed Tate (2000 WCPS) saying that a good speech includes head, heart, and humor. I opened the speech with the water's journey, from the Himalayas to the Indian Ocean. This is where my story began, from the Indian Ocean in Pakistan to the Stillwater Creek in Oklahoma. (When I said this while delivering the speech, the audience laughed; I wasn't expecting the laughter at this point.)

To get to my personal story, I wanted to bring up the subject of dating. I knew that simply mentioning The Dating Game was going to get a reaction from the audience. (And, it did.) This gave me a chance to bring up the comparison between dating and arranged marriages. When I mentioned that several families were interested in me marrying their daughter, I had to state why they would be interested in me. Was it because I'm tall, dark, and handsome? Mark Brown, in his winning speech talked about the tall, dark, and handsome prince. He got the audience to laugh when he went on to say, "I can relate to that." I got the audience to laugh (even though it took them a while) when I said, "As you can see, I'm not tall." (I also raised my hand above my head to indicate height and held that gesture until the audience laughed.).

Darren LaCroix talks about the tangent that leads the audience to laugh. In describing the American girl I met, I mentioned Cindy Crawford and Jennifer Lopez because the audience could relate to them. Since the obvious third character might be Britney Spears or Heidi Klum, I mentioned Martha Stewart. (The audience burst out in laughter.) I then went on to compare myself to the girl I met. Since I am from Pakistan and she is from Texas, I described us as chocolate and vanilla. Pauline Shirley, Past International President, suggested that I change chocolate to mocha. After I did that, David Hostler, a friend and mentor, suggested that I change vanilla to latte. (The mocha and latte humor went very well.) Since there is so much fuss about PC and Macintosh in television advertising, I used these for comparison and to get a laugh. (It worked.)

The statement, "Why do you want to marry someone who looks like that?" was delivered in a serious, whispering mode. During the first and second practice, the audience laughed. Cynthia Brown of the Park Central advanced Toastmasters club, who had heard the speech twice, pointed out that the audience laughed even though I didn't want them to. Instead of removing the sentence, I added the words, "It seems funny…now." (This got even a bigger laugh.). Since there was so much drama at home (in Pakistan), I decided to mention a

TV soap opera. I chose *The Young and the Restless*, because the audience could relate to it. The comparison of drama in real life and the soap opera made the audience laugh. When I included my mom as a character in my story, I remembered that she loved, I Love Lucy. I thought it would be funny to mention the show because Lucy was quite funny and all of us can relate to Lucy and Ricky.

Since we were married twice, once in Pakistan and once in the United States, I thought that mentioning two wedding anniversaries would certainly get a laugh. My final humorous line had to come before my message at the end. Jim Key (2003 WCPS) talks about call back to add humor. I called back "mocha and latte" that got the audience to laugh. Then, I added "frappuccinos" (my three children) for the humorous climax. (The audience burst out in laughter.). To my surprise, someone timed an audience's laughter during my speech – it was over 11 seconds long.

Jeff Johnson, Past District Governor, said to me, "You can be a champion, if we can get you there." When I walked onto the stage to deliver my speech, I wanted to win. After I walked off the stage and walked in front of Anne Barab, Accredited Speaker, she got up and hugged me. I knew then what many World Champions of Public Speaking have preached, "It's not about the trophy, it's about the audience." I am so thrilled to receive comments and emails from Toastmasters from Texas to Arizona saying, "The phrase, 'mocha, latte, and frappuccinos' is a big hit in our district." The humor worked! My family was not only a part of my speech; they also got to hear me speak for the first time in a speech contest. Yes, it's all about the audience.

The River of No Return

by Sarfaraz Nazir

The journey of a tiny droplet of water begins in the Himalayas, over twenty thousand feet above sea level. That droplet becomes a trickle, then a mountain stream, flowing into a broad river. The region of Pakistan beneath those great mountains is blessed with five major rivers flowing in close proximity.

When those rivers encounter obstacles, the relentless, raging rivers keep on pounding and pounding and pounding, wearing down boulders. Those five rivers eventually empty elegantly into the Indian Ocean. I see my journey's reflection in the water's journey. Once the water's journey begins, it moves forward with force; it NEVER LOOKS BACK.

Mr. Toastmaster, ladies and gentlemen, and anyone ever mesmerized by the power of water.

My journey began in the valley of the five rivers. My five sisters and I grew up fifty feet from the Indian Ocean. Everyday I saw, heard, and felt the roaring ocean. The waves would crest majestically and break with a thundering crash. I would stare at the horizon and ponder what marvels were beyond. This fascination drove me to leave home and arrive near Stillwater Creek in Oklahoma.

One day, as I trickled through the student lounge at Oklahoma State University, the TV blared a curious program, *The Dating Game*. Jim Lange asked "Who will it be--bachelorette one, two, or three?"

I thought, "What an odd ritual!" My marriage would be arranged by my family. Say what you wish—but I knew it would be a lot less painful than being rejected on *The Dating Game*. As for my wedding, I just needed to show up.

Several families in Pakistan were lined up, wanting me to marry their daughters. Not because they thought I was tall, dark, and handsome. As you can see…I'm not tall. Instead, they saw a better future in me. I often dreamt of my future bride - young, pretty, and intelligent. Then I met Linda.

No—you're going the wrong direction—Linda was a young, pretty, and intelligent, American girl. She was a blend of Cindy Crawford, Jennifer Lopez, and Martha Stewart. My world turned topsy-turvy. We were on the opposite banks of the river.

I grew up in Pakistan; Linda grew up in Texas. I was mocha, she was latte. I was a PC, she was a Macintosh. What a love fest. A candle was burning fervently for her in the cathedral of my heart. Remember when you first felt love in the air?

When Linda took me home to meet her parents, her mother pointed to a dark brown sofa chair and asked, "Linda, why do you want to marry someone who looks like that?" It seems funny … now; back then, it hurt.

With a wounded heart, I returned to Pakistan, with Linda by my side. We had barely landed when relatives began telling me "Going against our tradition by bringing this foreigner is a slap in our face." "Don't you know to stay away from those wicked women of the west?" When we arrived at our home, we faced more drama than *The Young and the Restless*.

My mom locked herself in her bedroom and cried, "Hi, hi, rabba." Which obviously meant, "What American grande latte has Sarfaraz been drinking? He needs a Pakistani bride." Linda locked herself in another bedroom and cried, "Pakistani bride? Over my dead body!" I was in the middle, drowning in their tears of love. My head and my heart were locked in mortal combat. Should I follow mom? Or should I listen to my heart? I was in a whirlpool of despair.

When water's path is blocked, it never gives up; it creates another path. I asked my five sisters to join forces like the five rivers and let me drift into a sea of tranquility. My mom did not speak English, but she loved *I Love Lucy*. My sisters told her that Linda was just like Lucy, zany but naive. "It worked for Ricky Ricardo, why not Sarfaraz?" After several days of consistent, persistent nagging, the wedding was on. And may I personally give thanks to Lucy and Ricky…

Since we were married across the ocean, we were concerned that the United States might not recognize our marriage. We remarried before a judge in Dallas. This means we have two wedding anniversaries. Yes, a few men just winced. Actually, it's a great luxury. If I forget the first one, I always get a second chance.

The doubt-masters had predicted, "This marriage won't last." You see, twenty-five years have sailed by since mocha and latte became one. We have three beautiful frappuccinos.

Ladies and gentlemen, I left the land of five rivers and the Indian Ocean, and made a home near the Trinity River between the Atlantic Ocean and the Pacific Ocean. I have been captivated by Linda and water. They showered me with three universal truths:

When there is a conflict between the head and the heart, the heart always wins. If you face obstacles, like water, never give up; create another path. And, once your journey begins, like the river of no return, GO FORWARD, NEVER LOOK BACK.

Analysis

"The River of No Return" is a delightful example of a speech intended to deliver a serious point, discussing serious issues, while softening the experience, and occasionally bringing greater emphasis to the point through humor.

Many of the tools of humor used in the more overt speeches in this book are used by Sarfaraz, but with a subtlety that does not diminish, but often enhances, its effectiveness.

1. Catchy Culture Comparison – Permission to Laugh
The opening of this speech starts with grand, sweeping descriptions and the introduction of the main theme: never look back. Just as the audience is comfortable with the tone, and believes it knows where the speech is going, Jim Lange and *The Dating Game* are mentioned. Humorous by its juxtaposition with majestic waves and the mention of Pakistan, listeners now know to expect the unexpected. References to *The Young and the Restless* and Lucy and Ricky Ricardo add to the pattern he creates.

2. Physical Humor – Laugh-Creating Gesture
When Sarfaraz mentions 'tall, dark, and handsome', he puts his hand over his head in a 'measuring position' used on children – evoking memories of 'must be this tall to ride this ride'. By picking out the 'tall' segment of this common expression, he avoids the common self-deprecation of denying he's handsome. By holding it long enough to get a laugh, he gives the audience both time to get the joke, and a combination of permission and imperative to laugh, warming them up for later humor. (Also a strong use of *Using Self as Punchline*).

3. Rule of Three – With and Without a Topper
As he mentions in the Author's Preface, the rule of three is prominent throughout the speech. Tall, dark, and handsome...I'm not tall. Young, pretty and intelligent...then I met Linda. Cindy Crawford, Jennifer Lopez, and Martha Stewart. Even while using phrases, the rule of three plays well: "I grew up in Pakistan; Linda grew up in Texas. I was a mocha, she was a latte. I was a PC, she was a Macintosh"

4. Dialog as Storyteller – It's About Characters
Emotional lines from his mother and his fiancée allow him to introduce concepts that could be seen negatively coming directly from him, but become humorous through the voices of the characters.

5. Voice of the Audience – Calling Out Humor
When discussing two anniversaries, he assumes the reaction from men in the audience. Even if no man actually winced, after hearing it mentioned, they may, or agree that they should have. Women in the audience take the twist on the familiar with humor as well, know men are the target of the joke.

6. Wordplay – Creating a Memorable Statement
Sarfaraz details his invention of 'mocha and latte, having three frappuchinos' concept in the Author's Preface. In addition to creating a memorable phrase, he creates an overall positive and humorous anchor in the minds of the audience immediately before closing with his main point. He takes advantage of the concept that people are more ready to learn after a laugh than at any other time.

It is important to recognize that this speech covers concepts as intense as love and marriage, internal family strife, cultural differences, stereotypes, determination and persistence. By using humor to soften and illustrate simultaneously, Sarfaraz creates a strong connection with his audience, and communicates strong themes without building walls between himself and his listeners. As speakers, we often face the challenge of discussing potentially controversial ideas – layoffs, discrimination, conflict, self-esteem, failure. Humor provides a release and a reframe, allowing your audience to consider what is being said without getting pulled down by its gravity. By building a bond with your listeners, by giving your discussion proper perspective through humor – they are ready to be called to action in the end.

Russ Dantu

Russ Dantu has been speaking professionally since 2001 and has entertained audiences in Canada, United States, Great Britain, Egypt, Mexico, and the Dominican Republic (ok, he actually sang in the Dominican during a karaoke night to a crowd of 1000+)!

A member of Vibrant Speakers & Wit Pleasure Toastmaster Clubs, achieving his DTM (Distinguished Toastmaster) award in 2002, he was judged one of the Top 20 speakers in Toastmasters International in 2009.

In the early years, many of his presentations focused on training trade show exhibitors, as he spent 25 years in that field. He gained a vast amount of experience in management, sales, and customer service in that time. Shifting his focus to teaching the art of public speaking (Speak Up) and customer service (The Path to Service Excellence Lies Within), Russ is passionate about helping people better their lives and their occupations through his keynotes and seminars.

He also is a corporate consultant with Times Two Gifts & Promotions. By selling promotional products, staff apparel, and unique gifts to his clients, Russ assists them in setting themselves apart from their competition. Russ lives in Calgary, Alberta, Canada and is happily married to his wife Sonia and has two grown children, Christopher and Carissa. When he isn't working, he enjoys playing golf and ice hockey (not at the same time), camping, and karaoke (ok, he's not a great singer, but he has fun)!

For more information about his programs or to contact Russ, please visit www.russdantu.com or email him at russ@russdantu.com

Author's Preface

Every fall, Toastmasters International hosts a humorous speech contest. Members, if they wish, can compete, and if successful, win at their club, area, division, and district. In District 42, which encompasses all of Alberta and Saskatchewan, Canada, there are close to 5000 Toastmasters making up over 250 clubs. I've always loved the rush of competitive speaking, and have found it to be the quickest avenue to self-improvement. On November 3, 2007, I was fortunate enough to win first place at the district level with my speech, *"The Big V."*

I do not consider myself a comedian or humourist, but have learned several techniques through humour boot camps, reading books, and watching those who have crafted this skill, which have helped me add humour to my speaking engagements. I also enlisted one of the best humorists I know, to help me "fine-tune" my speech, to take it over the top. That gentleman was fellow author, Palmo Carpino. The version you are about to read was the 5th edition, and while the mechanics and structure of the speech did not change much, having Palmo assist me in breaking down the speech and tweaking each area, it went from a very funny speech to having the audience buckled over in laughter. The opening was where I was really struggling. My original opening was mildly funny and clever but not a "WOW" opening. If you remember the television show, *Unsolved Mysteries*, hosted by Robert Stack, that was the scene I was trying to paint.

"Good afternoon, ladies and gentleman, the story which you are about to hear, which is of a delicate nature, will make the strongest of you cringe. Only the names have been changed to protect the innocent." It was alright but didn't grab the attention of the audience like a good opening should. While meeting with Palmo one evening, he suggested using life-threatening operations in my opening and then give the impression that they weren't serious in comparison to a vasectomy. The result was incredible. The audience lapped it up!

Many great ideas came from working with my coach, Palmo, but not all were used. Near the end of my speech, originally I speak about going home and being treated like a king. Palmo came up with an idea that I could take out a lamp shade and wear it like a cone around my neck signifying all I was when I got home was canine royalty! While I played with this idea, the use of props can be very tricky, and I was not comfortable using this prop when I practiced this at home, so it never made it to the speech.

Practicing this speech followed my usual format. Write it out, and then re-write it until I was happy, and then using a portable voice recorder so I could listen to it whenever I had time. Being in sales, I spend a lot of time in my vehicle. I would listen to it 7-8 times a day for about two weeks before each level of competition and then actually say it out loud in my vehicle (this always gets some strange looks from fellow drivers)! I use this technique to internalize the material, NOT memorize it. If it's memorized, it can often sound "canned" when you present it. While I do memorize my opening and conclusions, the rest of the speech is always internalized. This is somewhat difficult to do but when you master it, it allows you to play off of the audience's feedback and add material during your speech (time permitting).

For the use of props, I did a few practice runs at my Toastmasters' club and had several people watching to see how effective I was in the way I presented them. Ideas flowed and the way I used one of my props was changed significantly to give more impact. An example of this is when I'm on the operating table and the doctor walks in. If you've ever seen the movie *Braveheart,* where, near the end of the movie he is strapped down on the wooden plank and the executioner slowly rolls back the cloth to reveal all of the tools that would be used on him if he didn't pledge loyalty to the King, then you will see the visual I created while giving my presentation. Prior to this revelation, I simply took out the knife and held it up.

Through this I've learned that the easiest and most effective way to use humour is that of self-deprecation. When you open yourself up to the audience and show them your fears and downfalls in a humorous way, you will win their hearts, and still touch them with a serious message. Thus was the case with my vasectomy speech. For me, having a vasectomy was as traumatic as anything I have been through to date. I have never been that scared in all my life and thought I would probably die while going through it. In reality, it's a rather simple procedure with less than a 1% chance of anything going wrong (yep, I fell into the 1%, but that's a whole other story)! My doctor actually said that he had never seen anyone pass out during consultation for a vasectomy...before me – THAT'S how scared I was! My hidden message to my audience that day was that it's normal to experience fear. Having the courage to face your fears is what makes us stronger.

I leave you with this; there is no greater feeling than having a roomful of people buckled over with laughter because of your humorous presentation! I hope you enjoy the speech!

The Big V *by Russ Dantu*

Emergency Appendectomy? Hah! Piece of Cake!
Kidney Stones? A walk in the park!
A Tracheotomy using only a rusty pen knife and a Bic lighter?
Child's play! *(Chuckle)*.

The scariest procedure known to man is the vasectomy *(Laugh)*! How is it I can make such a statement? Been there, done that, left the building feeling a little bit different *(Walking across the stage, knees bent, with my hands crossing my lap - laugh)*!

Mister Toastmaster, fellow Toastmasters, welcomed guests, and any man who has survived the big V *(Chuckle)*!

I promise to tell the truth, the whole truth, and nothing but the truth, unless I think it really adds to my story! *(Like I'm in court with one hand on the Bible and the other hand open palm facing the audience)*. Only the names have been changed to protect the innocent - or because the official medical terms are way too difficult for me to pronounce *(Chuckle)*. This story may make some men squirm *(Hands shaking and looking at a male audience member)*. It may make some ladies laugh uncontrollably *(A villainous grin directed at a female audience member)*. It will make everyone feel the pain that I went through.

Several years ago, I came to a point in my life where I felt two kids were more than enough. It was time to consider having the operation. Now, you may be looking at me, thinking, "He's a pretty big boy, surely he can handle a little pain!" *(Chuckle)* I'm here to assure you that I am the biggest wimp in the history of mankind. When I have to go for a blood test, they have to lie me down on a bed and continuously talk to me or I pass out. If they sit me up in a chair and wrap that rubber band around my arm, it's all over! *(Chuckle)* Yes, I am the biggest chicken around.

When I needed to go for that mandatory consultation before the vasectomy, I wanted a doctor who was compassionate, who was kind, who had a steady hand *(Said with a look of fear on my face and a slightly shaky hand - chuckle)*!

A trusted friend of mine made me an appointment with a "European Specialist *(Said while using the quote symbols with both of my hands and raising my eye brows).*" The day came when I went for the consultation. I was waiting anxiously in the room when the doctor walked in, "Good morning, Mr. Dantu. I am doctor Chopemoff*!"(Said using a German voice - 10-12 second laugh.)*

"What was it about that name that made me cringe?" "So, you want to have a vasectomy, huh?" "Ah, I guess so." "Good. With this procedure there are a couple of times you will encounter pain. First is the needle freezing you. *(My hand gesturing like a syringe pushing the fluid out)*. Then I cut the tubes on each side. *(Hand gestures showing sharp cutting scissor motion)*. Now, drop your pants and let's see what we are dealing with here!" *(A scared look of astonishment on my face – 6-8 second laugh).* The next thing I'm told is that I had passed out. I was lying on the floor doing some sort of weird Elvis thing. *(I do my best shaky Elvis impression along with the curled lip – laugh).* When I came to, I was being helped up onto a table by the doctor and a nurse, "Mr. Dantu, in my 27 years of doing this, I have never seen anyone pass out during consultation. *(Chuckle).* You are not scared, are you?" Apparently, I freaked him out so badly that he prescribed me 4 pills to take before the procedure – VALIUM. *(Chuckle).* "Take two the night before and two the morning of." I was set. I wobbled out of the office and went home to relax. The night before my operation, I took two Valium and started to contemplate my future. Thoughts started running through my head. Strange thoughts. "Would people look at me differently? Would they know I was a Vasectomite? *(Chuckle).* "Hey, what's up, Vas?" *(Chuckle).* Would my voice change? *(Change voice to a high pitch when saying it – chuckle).* Would I have to run away and join the circus? You know, I'd be the freak in one of those sideshows. "Step right up and see…. Vasectomy Man!" *(Make my way across the stage and sound like a ring announcer and then place one hand across my lap, sheepishly smile at the audience and wave with other hand – 6-8 second laugh).* Ah man, I was a mess.

The day finally came when I had to make the trek to the hospital. I turned on the radio in the car to take my mind off of it. "Oh, I believe in yesterday. Suddenly, I'm not half the man I used to be…" *(I do my best Beatles singing impersonation – 8-10 second laugh).* I just couldn't win. I arrived at the hospital and was placed in the operating room. An attendant prepared me and finally the doctor walked in, "Good morning, Mr. Dantu, are you ready?" *(The "doctor" slowly rolls the towel open to reveal the knife and syringe).*

I looked him straight in the eyes and said with a broken voice, "yeah". He pulled out the needle – do you ever notice how BIG things look when you are scared *(I used the big end of a turkey baster with a 6" nail taped in the end of it-laugh)* and said, "Here goes the first pain." I squeezed the attendant's hand so tight, his eyes watered. I was shaking, then the doctor held up the knife. "Ahhhh, don't cut me, I'm not frozen yet!" *(I'm shaking my hands at the doctor and eyes are wide open with fear. The doctor is holding up a large butcher knife).* "Mr. Dantu, I've already finished, ha ha ha!" *(Laugh).* I started hyper-ventilating, "Help, I'm going to pass out!" The attendant told me to breathe deeply. "Buddy, I failed Le Mas class." *(Chuckle)* He quickly placed a mask over my face. It was happy gas. I was panicking; I was struggling not to be sick; I was floating on a big cloud – Wow, this is great! *(I start bouncing around the stage taking huge intakes of the happy gas and smiling).* Valium and Happy Gas are my friends! "I love you Doc, take your time!" *(Chuckle).*

From the time we started to the time we were finished, it was exactly 22 minutes. I had survived the scariest operation known to man. The Big V! I got up off that table and slowly walked towards the exit like a wounded John Wayne, *(try and walk like John Wayne - laugh)* "I'll see you around, doctor!" *(This was said in my best John Wayne voice).* I was instructed to go home, lie down and do absolutely nothing for the next few days. "Could I get that on one of your prescription pads, please?" *(Chuckle).*

Well, for me, it turned into a week.

Through my experience, I've come to realize that the world is a place of highs and lows, of give and take. You win a few, you....lose a few. *(Looking down and pointing to my lap area - laugh).*

One thing is for certain though – ask me if I'd do it all again, the answer is obvious ....Not a chance! *(Laugh).*

Analysis

In *"The Big V"*, we read another example of a speech written purely for humor's sake. The speaker's goal is to connect quickly with the audience, and build laughter throughout his speech. Within the 4 minutes 30 seconds to 7 minutes 30 seconds time-frame allowed, his goal is to create laugh after laugh, building to a crescendo ending. Keep in mind, this remains a speech, and is required to avoid becoming a series of stand-up jokes.

1. Humorous Open – Not the Opening Joke
By starting with dialog, speaking directly to the audience, the speaker connects quickly, using The Rule of Three with a twist immediately: Appendectomy, Kidney Stones, Tracheotomy. From the common to the painful to the absurd. By opening with energy and humor, he signals to his audience they've gotten aboard a fast-moving ride.

2. The Rule of Three – With and Without a Topper
'Truth, the whole truth, nothing but the truth' with the topper 'unless I think it adds to my story'. With longer statements as well: may make men squirm, may make women laugh, will make you feel my pain. The delivery of the triad cues the humor.

3. Creating Villains – Creating Humorous Conflict
Dr. Chopemoff (A James-bond type lampoon) comes in carrying a 'turkey baster' size syringe and a butcher knife. This exaggeration is common among most people, and we are able to 'see' his doctor as he tells us the story.

4. Using Self as Punchline – The Wimpy Man
The speaker paints himself as a weak and wimpy victim. He avoids the danger of making himself look truly weak by exaggerating the situation, and by appearing strong on stage as he makes fun of himself.

5. Props – Emphasizing the Humor
By actually using a turkey baster, the humorous image becomes all too real, and imaginations are creating pictures in their head right and left.

6. Wordplay – Words to be Remembered
Vasectomite. Good luck forgetting that invented word. Combined with *Innuendo* – 'you win a few, you lose a few', the speaker creates big laughs with a handful of words.

7. Exaggerating the Familiar – Even Familiar Taboos
Speaking of vasectomies is uncommon, and can create discomfort in audiences of all kinds. By taking us step-by-step through his procedure with humor, the audience quickly turns off their taboo radar, and trusts the speaker to bring them to an humorous conclusion.

8. Voice Characterizations - Humorous Impersonations
The speaker is impersonating both exaggerated characters and well-know stars such as John Wayne and The Beatles. This can be funny and effective even if done poorly! Be aware of how close you sound to your intended target voice, and decide which way to go - sincere imitation, or self-deprecating karaoke!

Knowing the audience, and their expectations, factors strongly into the success of this speech. There are few settings a topic such as this can be effectively and appreciatively lampooned. Try to apply the above humor tools to another medical procedure, or the dentists office, or take a quick left turn to your car's last oil change. How would you turn these everyday events into sources of humor?

By creating humorous anecdotes, you remain quick on your toes in any speaking situation, whether in front of 2000 Toastmasters giving a contest speech, or brainstorming with your management team on tight deadline. Mastering humor, as Russ shows in *"The Big V"*, is quite useful to take an uncomfortable situation and make it tenable, and even entertaining!

Kay Fittes

"Kicking Through Barriers to Your High Heeled Success"

Competency and talent alone aren't enough for women to succeed in the workplace, no matter what anyone tells you. Kay Fittes is a recognized expert in guiding women in breaking patterns of behavior that put them at a disadvantage in the workplace and showing businesses how to keep their best and brightest women. Since founding Strategies for Women's Growth in 1990, Ms. Fittes has lead more than 50,000 women in developing skills for career enhancement and leadership.

Kay brings a wealth of knowledge to her audiences, leading women in reaching the next level of success through the 3P's: powerful professional and personal esteem; powerful verbal and non-verbal language and powerful presentations and packaging. Kay's warmth, humor, rapport and examples of personal self-growth serve to inspire, entertain and challenge each audience member. With an insight to action approach, Kay Fittes takes audiences and workshop participants through an evolutionary, chameleon-like experience. They rarely leave the same as they entered.

Ms. Fittes is the author of How to Raise Your Self-Esteem: A Self-enhancement System for Women, Your Guide to Life-Changing Presentations, and the CD Panic to Power: Swift and Simple Speaking Strategies Anyone Can Use. She has written for AdvantageEdge and CincyChic magazines, as well as the Business Courier.

She has served as consultant and presenter to the business, medical, educational, and non-profits communities providing skills to such diverse groups as Ethicon, General Electric, Children's Hospitals, and the Ohio Department of Education.

Kay Fittes received her degree from the University of Tennessee, and is a member of the National Speakers Association; the American Society for Training and Development; the National Association for Self-Esteem; the Association of Female Executive; the American Association of University Women; and eWomenNetwork. She is past vice-president of the Ohio Council for Self-Esteem and past area governor for Toastmaster International. She has earned Toastmasters' Advanced Silver and Competent Leader designations and has won numerous speaking contests. In addition, she is a Certified Trainer and holds a Credential for Leadership Training. Kay also sits on several advisory boards for women's advancement. She resides in Cincinnati, Ohio with her husband, Barry.

Kay Fittes would love to keep you or the women in your organization in "Kicking Through Your Barriers to High Heeled Success", too! To book Kay for speaking, training or individual coaching call her at 513-561-4288, e-mail her at Kfittes@aol.com or visit her Web site, www.strategiesforwomensgrowth.com.

Are you "Kicking Through Your Barriers
to High Heeled Success" at work?"

Take the quiz at www.strategiesforwomensgrowth.com
to find out!

Author's Preface

Nothing resonates like reality, especially painful reality! *"Beware of Ladies' Night Out"* is a true story from my speaking and training career. It was first presented as part of a keynote I delivered at a Trainer's Institute in 2006, entitled, Surviving the Training Game. The keynote focused on steps speakers and trainers must take to prevent "shooting themselves in the foot" at presentations and burning-out in the field.

Keep in mind that I am not a humorist or comedian. The humor is derived from 1) reality, 2) pain, and 3) self-deprecation. It's funny because any presenter (speaker or trainer) could imagine being in a similar situation. There is always a point to my humor, never humor for humor sake. Since one division of my business is educating trainers, it's imperative that they understand the role of humor as a tool for engaging adult learners. Humor breaks down barriers faster than anything else I've ever tried, unless it's tears, of course. The late Dottie Walters, author of *Speak and Grow Rich* and owner of the Walters Speaking Bureau, said, "Begin with a laugh, end with a tear. That is profound wisdom from a great lady and mentor.

Since you are reading, instead of seeing and hearing this speech, you should also know that the humor is enhanced by my entrance. Following my introduction, I hobble to the stage covered with tattered, "bloody" clothes, to the tune of I Will Survive. It's quite the pitiful, yet comical, beginning. It is a great grabber that sets the tone for the entire presentation. As a four-foot, eleven-inch, 100-pound woman, (O.K. ladies, I'm slightly exaggerating the weight part but I am small), anything I can do physically to make an impact is crucial. Even in the twenty-first cventury, women still have to work harder to make an impact.

My company, Strategies for Women's Growth, specializes in "Kicking Through Barriers to Your High Heeled Success" in the workplace. Whether I'm speaking to professional speakers/trainers or to women in corporate America that give presentations as part of their job, the advice is the same: "Make an impact ASAP and find ways to use humor effectively."

Many of the readers of this book are speakers but some of you will be reading for the humor alone. I will tell you this keynote was given during one of the most difficult years of my life. As I went on stage that day, I was also awaiting word on two potentially life-threatening diagnoses for immediate family members. Humor got me through the day and ultimately, through that year of death, serious illnesses and painful loss. That is the power and healing property of humor. Where would we all be without it? Just remember, though, the Ladies' Night Out was in 1995 and the keynote was in 2006. Carol Burnett said, "Comedy is tragedy plus time." It was long journey to process this debacle, especially since my failure was in my own community. Now that I can share this ludicrous tale, audiences respond emotionally because they feel my pain and humiliation. Yet, the humor makes it palatable. That's a powerful lesson for all of us.

Let me close this preface by taking you back to the very beginning of my journey as a speaker. The funniest thing of all is the unlikelihood that I would be standing in front of any audience, period. The fact that I am a professional public speaker and trainer, the fact that I guide women in succeeding in the workplace and in becoming strong leaders, is nothing short of incongruous. Until the age seventeen, I was terrified of everything and everyone. It wasn't until I forced myself to take a public speaking class in High School that my "voice" began to slowly emerge.

If you are interested in hearing more about that process check it out in my *Panic to Power: Swift and Simple Speaking Strategies Anyone Can Use* CD at www.strategiesforwomensgrowth.com. There is good news for anyone there; your past does not have to equal your future.

Beware of Ladies' Night Out *by Kay Fittes*

Female audiences are fabulous -- they're attentive, they're supportive, they nod their heads in affirmation. Unless, of course, there are batteries, blow dryers or wine involved. Oh, behave yourselves! I'm talking about a school fundraiser, a Ladies' Night out, for heavens sake. Sounds like it would be a pretty safe venue for a speaker, right? Yeah, I thought so, too. I did my homework, like any other good little speaker would do--but... Can you spell D-I-S-A-S-T-E-R?

Why? I said I did my homework, I didn't say I got an "A". Apparently, I didn't do **all** my homework. (Shades of third grade all over again, I can hear Mrs. Blake right now. But I digress.) For this speech, there were critical questions I neglected to ask, and danger signs I ignored. Why is it that the lessons we need to learn the most frequently come to us in the most painful of ways? It doesn't seem to matter whether it's in speaking or in life. Perhaps it's because some of us are slower to catch on than others. O.K., I raise my hand in a solemn oath that I learned my lessons. So please, Universe, no more lessons like this one. It's taken me since 1995 to totally come to grips with this one. Told you I was a little slow to catch on.

Follow me back in time. It is 9:07 on July 19, 1995. The cavalry is on the other end of the phone line, the answer to my prayers. It's an opportunity to speak to 400 women for a hefty fee (hefty to me at that point, anyway). I have been transitioning from mixed gender audiences and focusing on women only in my speaking and training business. This opportunity could glean great referrals and give me the kickstart I need. Grandiose visions of every school district in America planning a similar event dance through my head. Heck, I'll settle for just all of Ohio. O.K., maybe Kentucky and Indiana, too. But the Universe has another plan.

There's good news and bad news. The good news is the event is in my own community, the meeting planner is the parent of one of my son's friends, an easier sell. The bad news is the event is in my own community, the meeting planner is the parent of one of my son's friends. Danger, Will Robinson! "You can't be a prophet in your own land." Bomb here and I'll be the talk of every coffee shop, beauty salon, and grocery store in the neighborhood. But I'm slow to learn, my greed glands swell up and I ignore the danger. We sign the agreement and charge ahead.

Again, as any good little speaker would, I perform my due diligence. I check out the venue in advance. The seating arrangement, the acoustics and the microphone all seem fine. The beginning and ending times are confirmed. The topic and title are chosen. I can already hear the thrilled audience applauding. Life is sooooo good.

At 5:35 on November 10, I arrive at the venue only to find:

Problem #1: To my horror, my previous room arrangement has morphed into Theatre-in-the-Round. There is **no front** of the room. Women to the right of me, women to the left of me, women all around me. Well, won't this be interesting! Now, I've never done theatre-in-the-round, have you? My immediate thought is, "My backside, not my best side." But I can cope. I'll just keep on turning throughout my presentation and hope the dizziness doesn't land me on that backside.

Problem #2: "Testing, one, two, three." I know I'm speaking but where's the sound? It's not weak, it's non-existent. The microphone that was just fine on the scouting trip has died an untimely death. No time for a funeral, where are the extra batteries? The venue co-coordinator gives me that Bambi-In-The-Headlights look that says "Batteries? No, I'm not packing any extra batteries." No problem! The former Girl Scout in me has kicked in and I have brought my own portable sound system. Are you impressed? Don't be. Seems I won't get the sound system badge after all, my batteries are dead, too. Extras? You're supposed to bring extras? So, I guess this means I'll just have to speak loudly, project effectively and hope they are a relatively quiet audience. Those of you that are snickering, I'm guessing you must have recall of the beginning of this speech. Which leads me to the next problem.

Problem #3: Do you remember part of this debacle was a result of not asking all the critical questions? I am standing in the room kicking myself for not paying more attention to the articles on diaphragmatic breathing and voice projection. Out of the corner of my eye, I see this band of women marching in with **thousands** of bottles of wine.... O.K., at least forty or fifty. Wine! No one told me there would be wine! No one told me there would be a Happy Hour **before** my presentation. Note to self, ask critical question #477: "What will be happening before my presentation?" Next time you give an important presentation don't forget #477. If the response is "Happy Hour", then ask, "Would that be a **sixty** minute hour?" If the response is affirmative... **RUN**! Run, Forrest run! Just imagine what 400 women on a warm up of wine sound like. So much for my hopes of a quiet audience.

Problem #4: Did I mention you need to ask **all** the critical questions? Right behind the wine toting troop were the.... hairdressers. No, no you didn't misunderstand me, I said hairdressers! Hairdressers with makeup... combs... brushes... and... **blow dryers**! That's right, blow dryers. In addition to the Happy Hour, we're having makeovers! And when will these lovely makeovers occur? During the presentation, of course.

Let's recap. I am speaking into a dead microphone...in Theatre-In-The-Round...with a content rich topic...to the tune of blow dryers in the background...to somewhat inebriated women...who just want to have fun. Now that's a formula for **disaster**.

What can you learn from my D-I-S-A-S-T-E-R? Remember these critical lessons the next time you present:

1. *Listen to your instincts.* When that gut-wrenching feeling first surfaced, the one that said, "These people only know me as Soccer Mom Extraordinaire, not an expert on issues for women," my response was "Shut up fool, there's money to be made here!"

2. *Match the speech to the objective.* The content-rich, though humorous speech, I prepared didn't quite match the attitude of "Let the good times and the wine roll... or flow, in this case." Years later, I know who I am. An after-dinner speaker I'm not. Ask yourself if you are really the right person for this audience and event.

3. *One disaster can't kill a career unless you let it.* Thankfully the very **next** day I attended the NSA Ohio Chapter's Speaker School. They were the voices of reason, hope, and analysis of this disaster. When all I wanted to do was curl up in a fetal position for the rest of forever, they made me look at why this happened and how to prevent this happening ninety-nine more times. This was a left brain endeavor, though. My right brain has taken years to process this fall-on-my-backside experience. Every time I talk about it, however, it gets easier and less painful. (No, I'm not paying you $100 an hour for being my therapist, even though I do appreciate your efforts.)

4. *Finally, do all your homework, just like my third grade teacher, Mrs. Blake, admonished.* Ask every question you can think of and then add at least seven more. Clearly it wasn't a public speaker who coined the phrase, "What you don't know can't hurt you!" Be smart. Don't "shoot yourself in the foot" at your next presentation.

Remember, women really are a fabulous audience. Just watch out for batteries, blow dryers and wine.

Analysis

Kay Fittes offers a serious speech designed to deliver serious strategies for speakers. It is heavily dosed with humor to both connect with her audience and anchor her points in the audience's mind.

The title itself signals the humor to come. *"Beware Ladies' Night Out"* would have had a tougher go if introduced as *"4 Ways to be a Better Speaker"* or *"Be Prepared"*. It implies something crazy or scary, or both, happened to a group of ladies' building suspense, and the expectation of craziness and scariness to come.

1. Rule of Three – Squared!
The speaker used this trick twice in the opening paragraph to set the stage, with: 'attentive, supportive, and nodding their heads...', as well as 'batteries, blow dryers, and wine'. Later she makes a point of how broad the embarrassment would be 'coffee shop, beauty salon, and grocery store'. She then combines two sets to extend her point of ridiculousness in her recap: without a microphone, theatre in the round, content rich topic, continuing to: inebriated women, blow dryers, just want to have fun.

2. Risky Entendres – To Connect
The audience members in this case are all women, and as a woman speaker, Kay takes a risk, throwing out the combination of batteries, blow dryers, and wine with the intent for a double entendre – then reeling them back with 'Oh, behave yourselves', which cues the audience that she was kidding, and builds an 'inside-joke' rapport with them.

3. Exaggerating the Familiar – Building Suspense
The night wasn't just bad, it was a disaster. It wasn't just a disaster, it was a D-I-S-A-S-T-E-R! By upping the level of disastrousness, she sets her audience up for something out of the ordinary, and based on her demeanor to this point, something

funny, as well. Later in the speech she refers to Critical Question #477. No one outside of NASA has a checklist this long, so in addition to being funny, it draws attention to her next point.

4. Sarcasm – Tread Carefully
In pleading with the universe to stop teaching her this lesson she has been trying to learn since 1995, the speaker can sound depressed, frustrated, angry, whiny – all downsides of sarcasm. When delivered with an upbeat or lightly resigned tone (use an exaggerated tone either up or down) it comes across with humor, and brings the audience closer in to the emotional state you are creating. A similar risk, that is less risky the more the bond is created with the audience, comes when she scoffs at her insecurity as a Soccer-Mom, proclaiming 'Shut up fool, there's money to be made here!'.

5. Double Meaning – Cuts Both Ways
The irony of the good news and the bad news being the same keeps the audience entertained and intrigued at the same time, and offers a reward for those who were thinking the good news wasn't so good before she said it out loud.

6. Catchy Cultural Reference – Across Generations
The speaker has three clear instances: Danger Will Robinson!, from the 1960's *Lost in Space*; Bambi-in-the-headlights look, bringing a clearer, Disney classic image to the typical deer-in-the-headlights look; and Run Forrest, Run – of course from the 90's blockbuster film *Forrest Gump*. While all are well-known, each hits a different age group square in the memory bank.

She transitions into her close with a callback to D-I-S-A-S-T-E-R, before finishing with a final reminder of batteries, blow dryers, and wine. These four, less than serious terms, all serve as reminders of the main points she gives to her audience. In a few days, they will still be thinking of these images with bemusement, and link them back to her intended messages.

Charlie Wilson

Charlie Wilson has been a member of Toastmasters for twenty years. He has won the District Humorous Speech Contest three times and the District International Speech Contest twice. He won the Region VI International Speech Contest in 2008 and went on to participate in the World Championship of Public Speaking. He has also won District contests in Evaluation, Table Topics, and Tall Tales. He has received two Distinguished Toastmaster Awards and served as District 13 Governor twice.

Charlie is the Professor of Mirth at Learning with Laugher, LLC, specializing in keynote addresses, workshops, and speech coaching and writing. His workshops include: Brain Aerobics, Creativity, Healing with Humor, Improvisation, and Investing.

Charlie is an Emeritus retiree from the faculty of The Pennsylvania State University. He is active in community theater and Rotary International.

Charlie can be contacted at www.learningwithlaughter.com, by email at charlie@learningwithlaughter.com, or by phone at 814-769-6041.

Author's Preface

I love trains and will ride one at any opportunity. The 2005 Toastmasters International Convention in Toronto provided one of those opportunities. I would fly to Vancouver take the train across Canada from there to Toronto.

As much as I love trains, I love reading even more so I stocked up on books and magazines for the trip. One of the magazines that I took along was *The Skeptical Inquirer*. One night, lying in the lower berth and reading prior to falling asleep, I turned to a pseudo-scientific article where the author presented 'convincing' evidence that some of the pictures in his house, despite being straightened in the evening, were tilted during the night by spirits that were trying to communicate with him. He presented charts and tables showing that these messages were encoded in which picture moved and by how much it moved. I laughed continuously while reading this well done spoof. How could I turn the idea into an original speech?

The disappearing sock has always bothered me and, to my mind, was a much more believable communication channel. I made some quick notes before nodding off. The next morning, over breakfast, I mentioned my concept for a pretty good humorous speech to my traveling companion. His response was "It ain't funny." That challenging remark gave me the spur to craft a contest speech.

It took a few trials to determine how many messages the spirits would send, what color of socks they would use, and the 'actual' messages that would be sent. I also had to pick a role, the nutty professor, for myself and come up with a bizarre conclusion. With a little polishing, *'Getting the Message'* turned out to be funny enough to win the District Humorous Speech Contest in 2005.

I have to agree with the often repeated statement that 'everything that happens in life is speech material.' Once, when I was changing the water in my aquarium, I spilled eight gallons of dirty water and half a dozen fish on the living room carpet. When I was lamenting this tragedy to my secretary the next morning, she laughed. The revelation hit – this is humorous speech material. *'Don't Get Hooked'*, a speech about the trials and tribulations of raising tropical fish, won the District Humorous Speech Contest in 1992.

Toastmasters gave me enough courage to do some acting in community theater. (I've acted in 71 shows since 1997.) My speech about the stress of my first audition won the District Humorous Speech Contest in 1997.

Audience laughter in reaction to what I say is the greatest high that I have ever experienced. I am sure that you find it just as rewarding. And competing in Humorous Speech Contests is the perfect venue to finding what is funny and perfecting your ability to incorporate humor in your speeches.

I hope you enjoy *'Getting the Message'*. Drop me a note if you do.

Thanks,

Charlie

Getting the Message *by Charlie Wilson*

<Dress in absent-minded professor garb.>
<Preset flipchart easel center stage, facing away from audience with top sheet blank.>
<Stay sitting until introduction by Toastmaster.>

<Stand up.> I've done it!

<Hurry to front of room with brief case tucked under arm. Papers are sticking out of case.>

After 47 years of painstaking research, I have solved the problem. And all the while there were many who thought me a wacky, old coot.

<Rush across stage to Toastmaster. Don't prewarn. The startled look on the Toastmaster's face gets a strong laugh.>

<Pump Toastmaster's hand vigorously.> Mister Toastmaster, fellow Toastmasters, guests.

Ever since I was a young man, I have been searching for some way to see into the future.

<Move right.> I have tried Ouija boards. *<Appropriate gestures.>*

<Move left.> I have used Tarot cards. *<Appropriate gestures.>*

<Move center.> I have consulted crystal balls. *<Appropriate gestures.>*

Nothing worked until now. I have discovered another dimension. And on the other side, there are entities that know the future and they are constantly sending us messages about what is to happen to us. It is really quite simple.

<Move flip chart to center stage and turn towards the audience.>

<Move to side of easel and turn page. Pull pointer from pocket.>

I call my technique *<point>* Super-Ordinary Communication from Kind Spirits.

Even after I discovered the existence of these spirits, I could not figure out how they were sending their messages. Then once day, as I was walking by the Laundromat, it hit me. *<Hit head.>* Wham! All along the secret had been right there, in my *<point down>* shoes.

How many of you, when doing the laundry, have had a sock disappear? Did you ever wonder where it went? Did you ever wonder who took it?

The kind spirits from the other side were sending you a message. You just couldn't read it.

That is why I refer to my technique *<point to chart>* as SOCKS for short.

<Put pointer away.>

82 Getting the Message   *by Charlie Wilson*

I know some of you are still skeptical. Well, let me show you some convincing evidence.

<Move to other side of easel and turn page. Socks are attached to page with velcro.>

I want to apologize for the condition of some of these socks. Government funding for this type of research is quite limited.

For example, *<pull green sock from chart>* we have the green sock, the money sock. Losing a green sock foretells the coming your way of unexpected money. Within two days of losing this sock's brother, I received a modest inheritance from my Great Uncle Lester. Modest but you can buy two Big Macs and fries for seven dollars. *<Show emotion while putting green sock in coat pocket with part dangling out.>*

<Pull brown sock from chart.> Next is the brown sock. It is the sock of disaster. The mate to this sock disappeared in March of 2000. In less than a month, the stock market crashed. Not only did I lose a sock, I lost my shirt. *<Pause. Emotion. Head shake. Put sock in coat pocket.>*

<Pull blue sock from chart.> The blue sock is the sad sock, the darker the blue the greater the sadness to come. Two weeks after the other half of this pair disappeared, TV Guide published the news that *Gilligan's Island* was to be cancelled. *<Emotion.>* Who among us can forget where we were the day that Gilligan left us. *<Shake head. Put sock in coat pocket.>*

<Pull red sock from chart.> The red sock is the celebrity sock. The loss of a red sock means that you are about to meet a famous person. Shortly after I lost the red sock, I met Wayne Newton. It was in Las Vegas. We were playing Black Jack together. *<Hold up hands.>* Well, maybe we weren't together. He was at the $1000 table and I was at the $5 table. But we were rubbing shoulders.

<Again with hands.> Well, actually, he was 35 feet away and our shoulders probably never touched. But he looked at me once, *<Pause.>* I think. *<Put sock in coat pocket.>*

<Pull polka dot sock from chart.> Now this sock ... *<Stop and stare at audience.>* I heard you snickering. *<Huff.>* I would never wear a sock like this. I borrowed it for this demonstration. *<Move away from audience and then turn back.>* Thanks, XXX. *<Where XXX is a well-known member of the audience.>*

<Scratch head with hand that has the sock in it.> Where was I? Oh, yes. The polka dot sock. Polka dots on a sock of any color, whether it be green, brown, blue, or red indicate that the prediction is a long-term one. The bigger the polka dots, the longer the wait. *<Examine sock.>* This one is a bit confusing with the dots of different colors and sizes but it was the only one HE (or SHE) had. *<Put sock in coat pocket.>*

<Pull pink sock from chart.> The pink sock is the canceller sock. It cancels a bad message. If you lose a bad sock – brown or blue – you must wear pink socks until one of them disappears so that disaster or sadness will not befall you. *<Put sock in pocket.>*

Two months ago, one of my brown socks vanished. Ever since then, I have *<show right foot>* worn pink socks. If you are having trouble seeing, feel free to stand up. Of course, I am always looking for money so ... *<Pull right pant leg higher to show green sock under pink sock.>* ...

<Pull orange sock from chart.> Finally, we have the orange sock, the two-way communication sock. If you have a question about the future that can be answered by a yes or no, you wash a pair of orange socks. If two orange socks come out of the dryer, the answer is no. If a single orange sock comes out, the answer is yes.

If you don't want to wait for a full laundry cycle for an answer, you can speed up the process by using my latest invention.

Getting the Message
by Charlie Wilson

<Take magician's change bag from briefcase One side is preset with single orange sock.>

I call this device the Kinetic Notifier of Express Edification for Super-Ordinary Communication from Kind Spirits or KNEESOCKS.

<Show bag to be empty. Take out another orange sock from briefcase.> I place these two orange socks in the empty device. *<Insert.>* I then ask a question. Let's see. *<Pace and ponder.>* Got it. Will I win the lottery tonight?

While we let the spirits do their work, let me remind you of the message that I want to leave you with today. Your future is not in the stock market. Your future is in the sock market.

Now ... *<Show single sock and empty bag.>* Oh, my goodness. *<Excitedly raise voice.>* I AM GOING TO WIN TONIGHT! I AM GOING TO BE RICH! EXCUSE ME! THERE IS A PORCHE DEALER JUST DOWN THE STREET!

<Begin to rush off stage. Turn and acknowledge the Toastmaster.>

Mr. Toastmaster.

Analysis

"Getting the Message" is a classic, Toastmasters-style, humorous speech. In addition to being strongly tailored to its venue, it contains many of the tools of classic vaudevillian hi-jinks, combined with the kooky playfulness of performers Danny Kaye, Groucho Marx, and Robin Williams.

1. Costuming – Dress for the Occasion
Showing up on stage as the 'nutty professor' type sets the tone immediately. People are immediately caught a bit off guard, allowing the suspension of disbelief to oil the gears for laughter. Taking it a step farther later in the speech, the speakers revelation of pink socks, and then green, makes the costume utilitarian as well as humorous.

2. Creating a Character – Fun and Funner
Taking the costume a step up by adding a real character vs. just the character of the speaker himself, again supports the suspension of disbelief. Setting up the situation of 'a wacky old coot' effectively prepares the audience for a complete performance of craziness.

3. The Unexpected – Surprise, Surprise!
By startling his introducer, the speaker confirms his declaration of being a 'wacky old coot'. The audience is as surprised as the 'Toastmaster'. The manic close of running off to buy a Porsche harks back to the initial shock, and creates a tidy package around an occasionally random main section.

4. The Rule of Three – Words in Motion
In building his character, Charlie professes to use 'Ouija boards, Tarot cards, and crystal balls', moving on the stage with each pronouncement. This use of the rule of three creates heightened expectation by the audience, and the physical movements add greater momentum to the humor to come.

5. Alphabet Soup – Acronyms to Remember

Taking a group of words and reducing them to their first initials has been a source of humor since President Franklin D. Roosevelt pushed the United States through the Great Depression with the introduction of dozens of acronym-titled programs in his 'New Deal'. By taking complicated terminology (Super-Ordinary Communication from Kind Spirits) and shortening it to S.O.C.K.S., the speaker takes a long yet funny name, and creates an ideal short name that people will remember for years to come. Extending the gag K.N.E.E.S.O.C.K.S. not only to call back to the original humor, but top it as well. Acronyms aren't easy, but when done right, create a memorable, and in this case, hilarious hook.

6. Catchy Cultural References

Always a great way to connect with the audience, the speaker refers to McDonald's, *Gilligan's Island,* and Wayne Newton – references most audience members know. For those that don't, it reinforces the age of the speaker, which in turn adds to the humor of the character created.

Any of these comic tools can be used in a corporate or otherwise public forum, as long as they support the premise. Coming out in costume can be wonderfully effective for setting the mood. Taking on a character for an entire speech comes with risks, but in the right situation, such as a roast, or a strictly entertaining setting, can pay off with easy laughter. Humorous acronyms are particularly useful in corporate comedy, and most companies are overrun with actual acronyms, and 'underground' acronyms. Doing your research to find out what those are will put you closer to your audience before you ever take the stage.

When you let the audience know you're there to have fun, they are more likely to have fun with you – so don't be afraid to borrow a few of the cues Charlie demonstrates in this piece of comedy in your future presentation, regardless of the venue.

Carrie Warren

Carrie Warren is a professional humorist for conference keynotes, after dinner speeches, client appreciations and has opened for best selling author Phil Callaway. Carrie inspires her audience to increase their 'LP' — Laughter Potential. By 'finding the funny' in everyday life, everyday life transforms into a fun, productive and profitable life.

Carrie has been a Toastmaster for 20 years and a dental hygienist since 1986. Some of her speaking clients include the College and Association of Registered Nurses of Alberta (CARNA), the College of Alberta Dental Assistants (the dental industry could use some lightening up!), Corporate Express, Grande Prairie Regional College and the Canadian Cancer Society.

Carrie's value goes far beyond laughter; she not only leaves her audience entertained but enlightened. Here's a quote from one of her speeches:

"A 'not-so-funny' event reminded me why humor is so important. I had taken my Mom to emergency. While waiting (and waiting) for the doctor, we started laughing and cutting it up. "Carrie," she said, "we better quit laughing so much or they'll think I'm not sick."

Then it hit me. Are only happy people supposed to laugh?

You must not wait to be happy to laugh but laughing can make you happy - even in an emergency room."

Through her personal stories about the follies of everyday life, Carrie helps her audience discover a most incredible power — the ability to laugh at themselves.

To hire Carrie as a keynote speaker for your event or for a humorous workshop, please reach her at the contact information below.

Carrie Warren
Grande Prairie, Alberta, Canada
Phone: 780-518-7255
www.CarrieWarren.com
Email: Carrie@CarrieWarren.com

Could your everyday life use some laughs? Sign up for Carrie's free e-zine "Crack Up with Carrie" at www.CarrieWarren.com.

"Embrace the Embarrassing and Make the Mundane Magnificent!"

Author's Preface

A horse named Flicka gave me my first taste of public speaking. "Straight from the horse's mouth," you may be thinking. It was because of Flicka that I ended up in a 4H speech contest in Grade 8. Afterwards, a judge named Paulette Patterson approached me. To this day, I remember her words: "Carrie, you sure know how to make us laugh."

Paulette's comments changed my perspective. I was an awkward, geeky teenager. Embroidered on the arm of many of my peer's coats was 'volleyball' or 'basketball' – a team sport they could be proud of and hear the cheers of the crowd. Mine said 'bowling'. In the midst of my awkwardness, I learned to look at life through 'humor glasses'. My mishaps became fodder for future speeches. Rather than berate myself, I learned to laugh at myself.

In a few pages, what you will read is no joke, no figment of my fertile imagination. Both events really happened.

However, there is a difference.

The bathing suit escapade happened in 1995. I was so humiliated I could not laugh about it. It was three years before I told the story to anyone. It was the family secret. When I finally told my best friends, they howled. This speech went on to win the Toastmasters 1998 Region IV Humorous Speech Contest in Omaha, Nebraska. It's become my signature speech. I've heard it said 'It's good to be remembered for something.' Seems my bathing suit speech left a lasting impression on a gentleman. Several years later, he bumped into me at a conference. "I don't remember your name," he said, "but when I close my eyes, I can still see you in your lime green bikini."

I asked him to open his eyes quickly. "It was lime green, but not a bikini, thank you very much!"

The airport incident took me no longer than 5 minutes to share. I grabbed the nearest stranger and spilled the beans. Three years versus five minutes. I had discovered the antidote to the sting of embarrassment. It was learning to laugh at myself and laugh sooner.

These stories get huge laughs. Why? The audience can relate to them. It may not have been a bathing suit; but it's been something. I take that 'something', expose it, embellish it and embrace it. In the end, the audience is not only entertained but more importantly, educated. Humor is fun, yet we're leaving its real power untapped unless we also use it as a medium to help drive home a serious message.

PS: Paulette, thank you from a girl who was hopeless and sports and needed something to be good at.

Carrie's Tips

The inspiration for my speeches come from my everyday life. This prevents the problem of using other people's material. The ability to laugh at myself and not be stifled by embarrassing moments has given me loads of material to speak about. I quite simply 'tell on myself' but never cross the line of putting myself down so that the audience feels uncomfortable for me.

In terms of presentation style, I'm outrageous and 'out there'. I've learned to encourage more laughter with pauses. Believe me, it's taken a l-o-n-g time to be comfortable with a five second and longer pause. During this pause, I may laugh along with the audience, mimic their emotion or simply repeat an exaggerated gesture. I find exaggeration works well for me. I may exaggerate with my voice or gestures such as rolling my eyes, raising or furrowing my eyebrows to give 'the look'.

In terms of writing, I picture myself on stage in front of the audience. I'm 'in the moment' on the stage as I write. I speak out loud various phrases whether it be imagery or dialogue and imagine the audience's responses to them. I speak it first, then type it on the computer. This exercise increases my creativity. I write and re-write, trying to nail the perfect word or phrase. The use of a story file is absolutely vital to capture my thoughts and ideas. My dental hygiene patients don't know it, but they're the guinea pigs for much of my material. I try several versions out on them. Often it's just a twist of a phrase or a word or a pause that takes it from funny to hilarious. We have a fun time together and they agree – it sure beats a flossing lecture!

As a speaker, I firmly believe your message has the ability to change a person's perspective on life. After an engagement, a sharp-looking middle aged lady came to me and said, "I sure wish it was me in that bathing suit." "Whatever for?" I asked. "I need to learn how to laugh at myself just like you." If my bathing suit has helped her learn this valuable life lesson, wearing it and sharing it has surely been worth it.

Happy writing and speaking to you!

Carrie.

Laughing in Everyday Life

by Carrie Warren

Are you a people pleaser? For all I know, you may be here today just to please someone. I'm guilty. In fact, I'm a self-proclaimed People Pleaser. How bad am I, you're wondering? I wanted to help out my newly-graduated OBGYN, so I considered getting pregnant a third time just to give him business.

But one experience changed all that and let me tell you, my people pleasin' days are over.

Family reunions. Don't you just love them? Come every family reunion my sister-in-law insists, "You HAVE to swim with us. The family reunion just won't be the same without you."

Now I don't really like to swim, so I came up with a foolproof plan. I would conveniently forget my bathing suit at home – everytime.

At the last reunion, I had just finished presenting my excuse with great emotion.

"The family swim! Drat. I was so looking forward to it. But--- I forgot to bring my swimsuit."

My sister-in-law was not to be outsmarted. She smiled sweetly and pointed to a sign "RENTALS."

Now I've rented a movie, a car, even a rototiller, but a swimsuit?? *(pause (P))* Have you ever rented a swimsuit? *(Pregnant pause (PP) Look at one person in particular chosen ahead of time and call by name ie a dignitary, the office clown, etc.) (Person's name)*_____ you have? *(depending on the crowd and the laugh to this person's name, I may say, "And you're wearing it now?)*

Obviously there was only one thing for me to do.

"One rental please," I whispered to the cashier, a size 2 tanned blonde bombshell straight out of Vogue magazine.

She took one look at me. "LLLLARGE!" she yelled to the girl at the back.

To get even I wanted to yell back, "EXTRA SMALLL!!" But it didn't seem to have nearly the same impact.

I waited and waited. And then I waited some more. I became suspicious. If other people rented swimsuits, what was taking so long with mine and hey, why was I the only one in line?

I soon had my answer when she returned, gagging and sneezing and clutching two misshaped bundles covered in dust.

"There must be some mistake," I told Extra Small. "I asked for rentals, not relics."

Extra Small was not amused, but then again, by this time neither was I. These suits were World War II relics. They featured a corset to fight the battle of the bulge *(gesture squeeze at waist)*. Even the top was built with 'heavy artillery' in mind *(gesture heaviness under the bust)*.

Now the smart person would have quit right here. What made me continue? People pleasing. Years and years of people pleasing had made me plain foolish. Unable to think for myself, I was about to hit the water like a giant buoy.

At least I had a color choice. Royal blue or lime green. Now which suit do you suppose fit me best? The lime green one of course. Bill Cosby could have used me in a Jell-O commercial. (P)

You know how most swimsuit styles start at the shoulder and end at the top of the leg? Well, this World War II suit had either become battle weary or got itself run over by a tank. Or both. It started at my shoulders all right, but then marched on down my trunk and past my thighs before coming to a halt at – my kneecaps.

The corset, however, refused to admit defeat. (P)

Have you ever seen a sausage in its casing? (P)

Have you even been a sausage in its casing? (P)

With my considerable cleavage squeezed up to meet my double chin *(gesture)*. I now knew what that sausage felt like. (PP)

Out of desperation comes hope. "Maybe it doesn't look as bad as it feels," I lied to myself. Since I forgot my glasses, I shuffled to the mirror for a closer look. *Do an exaggerated shuffle.*

I felt like the woman in that old 1960's song – the one getting all the attention. You know the song: Sing it!

"One, two, three, four. Tell the people what she wore."
"She wore an itsy, bitsy, teeny, weeny yellow polka dot bikini."

Oh, I was going to get their attention all right.

"She wore a lime green tent that she did rent, so long and tight her knees were bent." *Sing it off-kilter*

Then I remembered Mom's simple solution for anything that was too long. "No need to hem dear, just roll." Didn't matter what the garment was - pants, shirt sleeves, even underwear. I see _____ *(person chosen ahead of time to have fun with)* just got a brain wave here. If it was long, Mom rolled it.

Finally, I was ready to make my debut. My rolled cuffs were in place and the bust support was incredible. NASA could have used the foam cup liners as rocket boosters. (P) *Gesture to bust or say 'Pu-ching!!'*

1.In my defense, it's not as if I didn't give people fair warning. My 42 Double D's stood at attention more firmly than they have had in years. I looked like the front of those military jets - the ones that could poke an eye out. (P) Let's just say my bust came around the corner a full three seconds before I did. *(PP – perhaps replay the gesture while the audience laughs)*

I stood at the side of the pool and squinted at the crowd. "Where is that husband of mine?" I grumbled. "Kevin knows I can't see a thing without my glasses." *Exaggerated squint as I peer around*

Apparently, that's what he was counting on. *(PP nod my head as audience laughs)*

There is a certain hush when people are in awe. Convinced I was the object of their attention, I jumped into the pool. Now, let me ask you, "What happens to a 5'4 woman who takes the plunge in a rolled up rental?"

Just like the Titanic, I took on water. (PPP)

Parents were shouting to their small children, "Get out of the water! Get out of the water now!!" *(make the 'do do, do do' sounds from the Jaws movie)* And just like the Titanic, that suit went down in history, never to surface again. (PP) I have nieces and nephews who have not yet fully recovered from what they saw. (P)

My sister-in-law was right. The family reunion wouldn't have been the same without me. (P - *while nodding*) At least one good thing came out of it. She's never asked me to swim again, probably for fear I'd say yes.

I'll tell you, if it's not one thing, it's another.

Just when I got people pleasing out of my system, along came embarrassment.

Is it just me or do you feel like embarrassment hunts you down? *(Nod in agreement and perhaps choose an audience member by name).* Just when I think I have it all together, WHAM! I'm blindsided by an embarrassing situation.

Oh it's easy to laugh when the joke's on someone else, but how do you laugh when YOU'RE the one who's embarrassed? The words of my friend Rhonda Jean changed my perspective. Rhonda Jean says, "THE PERSON WHO GETS THE BIGGEST KICK OUT OF ME IS ME."

It's that simple. Life happens. Decide to get a 'kick' out of yourself.

I had a chance to put this theory to the test in the Edmonton International airport. Security Susie waved her magic wand. You know the routine. My watch beeped, my rings beeped. Even my underwires beeped (P) No big deal until….

"Ma'am, REMOVE your belt."

I don't know about you, but I'm not used to removing my belt in public. I had on my new low rise jeans. The problem? I had on high rise undies. (P) *Gesture pulling up undies under armpits while squatting down.* When that belt came off, three inches of pink lace control top was unleashed. (P) *Loud raspberry blowing sound for unleashed...* It could be seen 30 feet away with the naked eye.

STIIINNNNNNGGGGGG! Oh, the sting of embarrassment hurts. "Ma'am, arms up and turn around," the attendant barked. *Do the arms up gesture with quaking and 'deer in the headlights' look*

Now I'm in Edmonton, but live five hours away in Grande Prairie. What are the chances that I know the next person in line? Apparently, pretty good. (P)

"Hello, Dr. Muir." (*wave with look of disbelief*) It was my gynecologist. (PP) Yes, the very man I nearly had child #3 for. (PP) *If there has been a squeal of laughter, I've sometimes said, "Oh, you've run into Dr. Muir too?"*

My old friend embarrassment was taunting me again. Do I try to escape embarrassment or embrace it? I thought of Rhonda Jean. Now would be a good time to get a 'kick' out of this!

I cleared my throat, looked my gynecologist straight in the eye, pink lace undies and all and said, "Well, Dr. Muir, I guess you've seen me without my belt before." (*Big laugh here – feel comfortable pausing – count to 5*)

The embarrassment melted away. It simply could not withstand the healing wave of laughter.

When I woke up that morning, I didn't know my underwear would be exposed in an airport in front of my gynecologist. When you wake up tomorrow, you don't know what you'll face. (*Big pause for effect – hold gaze for a second or two with a couple audience members*)

To be successful in life, we're told to confront our fears, to rise above our failures, but what about our embarrassment? You may be tempted to cast off embarrassment as a frivolous emotion just because you've laughed at my stories. But embarrassment can stop you on a dime. Its sting can paralyze you and you can become too afraid to try anything new. *(P for effect – audience is silent)*

Have you ever said, "I could have died of embarrassment?" Sadly, some people live their lives this way – quietly, held back.

Embarrassments are an essential ingredient in life. When they happen – and they will – you may want to run, hide or pretend it never happened. But that merely buries a pain that you may carry for the rest of your life.

Please don't hesitate to embrace the embarrassing. Who knows, maybe your gynecologist will be there to witness it!

Analysis

Laughing in Everyday Life is a wonderful example of an entertaining speech wrapped by a motivational message. Carrie's message to 'face our embarrassments' is a tremendous life lesson, and is proven with her humorous anecdote delivered with virtually every humor tool in the book – even THIS book!

1. Self-Deprecating Opening
A quick introduction to our speaker as a 'People Pleaser', with the first laugh coming after a classic 'How Bad Am I' reference, punctuated with her consideration of getting pregnant just to give her OBGYN business.

2. Sarcasm - Twisting Negativity
The dialogue "Drat, I was so looking forward to it" is dripping with contradictory language vs. meaning. Written in conversation mode to the point we can hear her villainous tone of voice.

3. Rule of Three - Toppers and Pauses
Movie, car, rototiller (this gets the first laugh) (pause) but a swimsuit? A textbook list of real items with an oddball thrown in, then enhanced by the incredulous-toned question as a topper. The delayed rule of three works later in the speech: battle weary or got itself run over by tank. (Pause) Or both. Timing and tone are crucial here. The set-up is enthusiastic and straightforward. After it sets in as humorous, the "Or both" comes in a lower tone, almost as a sidenote, pushing the laughter yet again.

4. Creating Villains – Creating the Heroes
By identifying characters by characteristics instead of names, the audience gets both a clear and funny picture of Carrie's Bombshell Renter XXXsmall and Security Susie – we

reference the images in our own minds, and increase the joke internally. We also begin to see Carrie as a heroic underdog.

5. Using Self as Punchline
Contrasting herself as XXXtra large, suggesting a smart person would have stopped (but not her), describing herself as a gigantic buoy, and admitting that the reunions not the same without her are references that evoke sympathy, trust, as well as laughter. We are rooting for the speaker throughout the speech.

6. Kitschy Cultural Reference
Few speeches can successfully mention both Bill Cosby's Jell-O commercials and World War II's Battle of the Bulge. Carrie's references cross generations, effectively getting her point across.

7. Humorous Imagery
This speech is ripe with imagery: "Seen sausage in its casing, been sausage in its casing, [now knows] what the sausage felt like" creates a clear picture, while being delivered in deliberate cadence. "NASA foam cup liners as rocket boosters, military jets that could poke out an eye – my cups came around the corner three seconds before I did" again gives us exaggerated images to reference, as does: "Titanic taking on water" set up another classic question "do you know what happens when", followed by the over the top results: "get out of the water now! Nieces and nephews haven't recovered - high-rise undies, three inches of pink lace control top was unleashed, could be seen 30 ft. away with the naked eye!" The avalanche effect of ludicrous imagery creates momentum and builds laughter to a crescendo.

8. Silly Singing
Carrie is unafraid to take chances, singing: "itsy bitsy teeny weeny yellow polka dot bikini", topped with her with own lime green tent verse. Adding song to a humorous speech can be risky, but with risk can come great reward. You don't have to be a great singer, and sometimes it helps if you are not!

9. Sound Effects
"Pu-Ching", the loud raspberry, and "STTIIINNNNNNNN-NGGGGGGGGG!" all add another layer to the story, putting us in the scene by sound as well as sight.

10. Callbacks - Funny Once, Funny Twice
In her pre-close, Carrie again references her gynecologist (a funny word in and of itself) and potential child #3, followed by the big line "I guess YOU'VE seen me without my belt before" (vocal delivery is vital in this moment), and then ends the speech again with her last line callback to her favorite doctor.

While the speech is funny throughout, Carrie still hits home with a strong instructional point – embrace the embarrassing. She pushes her humor to the breaking point, without ever crossing boundaries for typical corporate taste and sensibilities. The potential to move to crassness is both a challenge and a benefit. Even as Carrie worked to maintain a professional demeanor in her images and language, the audience may have been listening closely to hear if she crossed a specific line of decency. Even riskier is the fact that that line is different for all. That small sense of tension actually helps the speech, keeping the audience engaged.

Corporate humor is an expanding market, particularly as the news is dominated with doom and gloom reports. If you typically speak in motivational terms, recognize the strenth of this speech is not just the humor, but the uplifting overall message almost hidden within the humor. Carrie's speech is a dynamic example of what can be accomplished when the tools of humor are applied to a straightforward life lesson.

Terry Canfield

Terry Canfield is a Professional Trainer, Consultant, Speaker, Author, and Stand-up Comedian.

Drawing upon his 25+ years working as a Paramedic/Firefighter, Terry uses his experiences to entertain and educate his audiences.

Humor has been some of Terry's most potent painkillers and has calmed more than one calamity. In his speech "Rules To Live By When Calling 911!" Terry takes a lighthearted approach to some of life's ups and downs.

With this book you can become a "healer with humor". After all, it's the only form of medicine you can practice without a license!

Terry Canfield
"The Medic of the Masses!"
See why at:
www.TCanfield.com
(509) 230-8197

Author's Preface

Injecting your presentation with humor, appropriate humor, *appropriate humor that makes a point,* is so powerful, lives and lands have been won and lost by its use. I like to use humor for several reasons...

First, it gives me immediate feedback as to how "with me" the audience is. Secondly, humor accesses a couple of critical areas in the cerebral cortex area and Wernicke's Area, and these two gatekeepers are vital for making my message meaningful and memorable. And thirdly, I would much rather have a good time at a presentation, whether I'm giving or receiving, than be part of a talk that's so dry you swear you're in Death Valley. It's just more fun!

There are numerous techniques to employ for generating humor but all of them boil down to creating the same phenomenon - getting the listener moving in one direction then changing their direction like a weather vane in a hurricane. The more dramatic the change of direction the more intensity and therefore impact you'll have. But not all intensity and impact is humorous.

I developed a class, primarily for corporate clients, to measure an atmosphere of humor in their organizations or their lives called *"How To Increase Your Health, Wealth, And Stealth Through Humor!"* In this program I introduce a yardstick for measuring your slapstick. It's called the **P.R.A.I.I.I.S.S.E.E.D.D.** method. I will briefly describe it for you here.

There is a certain amount of subjectivity to this rating system. So I always advocate having someone who is not emotionally connected to the issues or pursuing some sort of an agenda do the rating.

P is Polarity (positive vs negative). Is the humor in question positive or negative in nature? Most humor has some kind of negativity connected to it, but that isn't necessarily a bad thing.

R is Relationship (others, God, self). Here is the spectrum of relationships: God, Humanity, Community, Acquaintances, Friends/Enemies, Family, Self. Except for God I have moved from the least personal to the most personal. God is treated as a vertical relationship while all others are treated as horizontal relationships.

A is Activity (external, i.e. practical joke vs internal, or thought provoking). Just how physical is the humor? As the saying goes, "It's all fun and games until someone loses an eye!"

I is Intensity (outrageous or out like a light). Is the humor spectacular or subtle?

I is also "Intent City" (consistent vs. contradictory). What is the intent of the delivery? Is the humor meant to incite a riot or provide comedic insight?

I is also Impact (low, medium, or high). How was the humor received? This can be quite different than the intent.

S is Security (secure vs. insecure). Does the humor reassure or invoke feelings of emotional loss?

S is also Safety (danger vs. no danger). Is there any physical harm involved in the humor, such as a mocking dare.

E is Entertainment (judged by the audience). This is actually measuring the amount of "humor" but is also very subjective.

E is also Educational (critical behavior change necessary for performance). Think here of making someone the butt of a joke during Basic Training in the military to increase their performance and therefore their ability to be effective during, or at least survive, combat.

D is Direction (moves audience together or apart). Is the effect of the humor one that bonds, or one that bombs, relationships?

D is also Duration. Even low intensity humor can accumulate and create significant impact over time.

These parameters are all somewhat subjective. Using predefined comparisons helps quantify these characteristics. but it may very well require a consensus to determine each individual characteristic.

The purpose of the **P.R.A.I.I.I.S.S.E.E.D.D.** system is to begin to quantify humor in an attempt to evaluate a given situation and determine the appropriateness of the humor involved. The circumstances surrounding the incident will have a tremendous amount of influence on this determination as well.

Another important part of humor is to become accountable for our own feelings. Humor does not MAKE us laugh, or mad, any other description you want to insert here. WE choose to respond to humor based on the our experiences and personality. But, it is still we who do the choosing. In short, we would all do better if we expanded our own sense of humor, especially when the humor is directed toward us personally or any other group with which we identify.

Humor is a source of energy as invisible as atomic attraction or as obvious as a nuclear detonation. The creator of the humor only has so much control but with practice perception and patience the ability to plan the results of humor become much more predictable.

Above all... HAVE FUN FOR EVERYONE!

If you want to view a video of the speech that is presented here click on this link or go to: http://www.whoisterrycanfield.com/Rules/

Rules to Live By When Calling 911

by Terry Canfield

People love to talk about the "Good Ol' Days", but you know... the good ol' days weren't always that good!

Look at Emergency Medicine for example. Did you know that prior to the 1970s most of the ambulance companies in the United States were owned and operated by... funeral homes?

Now there's kind of a conflict of interest here, "take 'em to the hospital? Take 'em to the funeral home. Hospital? Funeral home. They get the money. We get the money. They get the money...

"Sorry pal... doesn't look like you're going to make it.'"

You could tell by the kinds of vehicles we drove! This is what an ambulance looked like back in the 40s, 50s, and 60s... It's a hearse painted white.

If you were still alive when you got to the hospital, your chances of survival improved significantly. The engine compartment is bigger than the patient compartment and it's a good thing because there wasn't a whole lot of patient care going on back there in those days. Our motto back then was, "You fall, you call, we haul and that's all!"

108   Rules to Live By When Calling 911   *by Terry Canfield*

So they changed all that. They sent us to school, taught us how to start IVs, give you drugs, shock the stuffings out of you with that cardiac defibrillator. In fact, that was the first three months of Paramedic training... learning how to say cardiac defibrillator!

Now our motto is, "You fall, you call, we'll stall and maul before we haul!"

Well tonight I want to give you a few things to think about the next time you get the urge to call 911.

Rule number one, "Don't bite the hand that bleeds you!" Now this is easier to do than you might think. We realize when you're hurt or sick you don't feel well, a little grumpy... half the time you bite our heads off! That's OK; there is one unpardonable sin, however, and that's if you call me "an ambulance driver."

Now being the truly dedicated professional that I am, you'll never see me grimace or grit my teeth. But before you know it, you'll wonder why it feels like I'm drilling for oil in your arm... or why it takes five needles to start one IV.

Rule number two, "If you're going to be stupid... you'd better be tough!" Now this rule was written specifically for females between the ages of fifteen and twenty five... and ALL males! Look at Evel Knievel... The man has made millions of dollars... for his team of orthopedic surgeons!

Rule number three, "Paramedics get paid for what they know... not for what they do!" What this means is, if you have a problem with any of the Three "P's" That's piss, poop, or puke... we're not going to clean it up. We'll get you to the hospital just as fast as possible because we feel that's why nurses get paid, "The Really Big Bucks!"

Rule number four, "Caution... cell phones maybe hazardous to your health!" And this has nothing to do with ear cancer. Recent research has confirmed that cell phones SUCK every ounce of common sense out of your head! We get calls for people changing a flat tire, people laying down... in the park... on a blanket, and we always ask the caller, "Did you stop and see if they need our help?"

"Noooooooo"

So we always tell the caller, "We'll be right there... TO CONFISCATE YOUR PHONE!"

Rule number five, "Don't take this life too seriously... but don't EVER take it for granted!" Over in Eastern Washington we have a city named Omak... and these people know how to party! They have a weeklong celebration called the Omak Stampede. And at the same time, they have this thing called a Suicide Race!

Now I don't know about you but it sounds to me like the first person to kill themself wins! I don't know what first place gets... but it's not enough!

Well ladies and gentlemen, Dr. Samuel Shem said it best in his book *"The House Of God"* when he wrote, "When you're dealing with a cardiac arrest... the first pulse you check, is your own!"

And if it's there... Thanks God!
And if you have to... call 911.
But remember this... If you wake up, and you're looking at me... It's a bad day!

Ask my Ex!

Analysis

"Rules to Live By When Calling 911" is an excellent exercise in revealing the humor in what most people view as a serious undertaking – the life of an EMT. The speech is specifically designed to entertain the audience, with little meat for the the listener to have to digest. An excellent dessert offering. While it is short in length, it is long in technique, utilizing well several tools mentioned to this point, and adding a couple of its own.

1. Wordplay – Turning Phrases Inside-Out
By opening with "The good old days weren't all that good", Terry begins his speech by setting us up for a lesson in history, and suggesting we refocus our version of reality. The quick set-up may or may not result in a laugh, but it certainly sets the audience up for humorous sarcasm.

Phrases such as "you fall, you call, we haul, and that's all", "you fall, you call, we'll stall and maul before we haul" and keeps listeners on their toes to keep up.

2. The Unexpected – Reality Can Be Surprising
With his first revelation, that ambulance companies used to be run by funeral homes, humor begins to flow naturally through the speech. The topper comes when Terry reveals the car model of the early ambulance as being, in actuality, a hearse.

3. Dialog – Giving Characters the Punchline
Starting with the original ambulance driver persona debating "They get the money, we get the money", continuing to "We'll be right there, to confiscate your phone", Terry goes from 'speaker mode' to 'EMT' in seamless fashion.

4. Exaggerating the Familiar – Adding Laughs to the Linear
As Terry advances the storyline, he keeps what could be dry narration moist with humorous exaggeration. Lines like

"shocking the stuffing" and "three months...to learn to say defibrillator" keep the audience chuckling as they follow him through the speech.

5. Sarcasm – Revealing Reality Through Humor
The speaker is accomplishing a dual purpose with his rules to consider before calling 911. Using sarcasm, he keeps the mood light, but simultaneously reveals a bit of what goes on inside of a typically stereotyped EMT's head as they answer a call. This window to the inside both educates and connects with audiences of every type, except, perhaps, his employers.

6. Catchy Cultural Reference
Terry admonishes future patients by bringing to mind the image of Evel Knievel, stating he's made "millions of dollars....for orthopedic surgeons".

7. Edginess – How Far Should You Push?
Knowing your audience helps, and setting yourself up is crucial. Terry is a large physical force, who is telling real stories from his perspective and experience. While he may push the boundaries of taste with lines such as "Piss, puke, and poop", and "we feel that's why nurses get paid", these lines also come with authenticity, and actually mirror the jarring nature of his subject matter.

8. Tailored Humor – Close to Home, But Not Too Close...
This version of the speech was delivered in Washington State, giving Terry the perfect opportunity to poke good-natured fun at a local town and their tradition of a suicide run. Given the opportunity to research locales, it is likely he can find similar events near wherever he speaks, while still using Omak, WA as an emergency back-up by simply referring to his 'old stomping grounds'. Using a local reference is a strong way to connect with your audience, as long as you are referring to a common target amongst your listeners.

9. Rule of Three – With a Topper

The speech closes with a classic rule of three – And if, And if, But – essentially a sales tie-down. Get the audience to nod there head twice, then throw out the change-up: "If you're looking at me...it's a bad day!" Refusing to end there, he goes for one final laugh: "Ask my Ex!" This is in keeping with the edgy nature of the speech, and with the proper facial expression and preceding pause, will certainly keep this EMT's audience in stitches.

This speech works well on its own or within a longer keynote offering. It can easily transition from speech to stand-up, and displays flexibility in the type of humor used. With a few adjustments, it can just as easily entertain architects or auto mechanics, senior staff or stay-at-home mom's, doctors or day-workers. By giving a serious subject a humorous slant, Terry proves that even in moments of stress, laughter is the best medicine.

Douglas Wilson

Douglas spent over 12 years in the United States Air Force, traveling to such exotic places as Texas, California, Montana, Guam, Okinawa Thailand and Arkansas, where he first discovered Toastmasters.

After leaving the Air Force he enjoyed exercising his creativity as a freelance photographer specializing in outdoor and natural light portraiture.

He has also been a radio/paging communications specialist - home re-modeler - student - teacher — salesman - and computer consultant. During this latest incarnation he had a weekly talk show on a local radio station for over a year discussing computer technology issues.

He and his wife JoAnn have been together over 27 years and own and operate their Network Marketing business in Sumter, South Carolina. Their focus is on Health, Nutrition and Life Extension with the Shaklee Corporation, Pleasanton, California. Douglas is also a speaker and coach and is developing several internet marketing projects.

Their son, Ryan, recently graduated from college with a degree in Computer Technology. Douglas also has a daughter, Tamara, who teaches 4th Grade in Blytheville, Arkansas, where she lives with her husband, Troy, and two children, Tiffany and Tanner.

As a Toastmaster, he has served in all Club leadership positions, as well as Area Governor for four years (Area Governor of the Year in 1998-99) and Division Governor for two years (Division Governor of the Year in 2000-2001) and was Outstanding Toastmaster of the Year in 2003-04.

Douglas began competition in 2003 placing 2nd in the District 58 Speech Evaluation Contest in 2003 & 2004. He won the District 58 Humorous Speech Contest in 2005 and placed 2nd in the World Championship of Public Speaking in 2006.

Douglas is a strong believer in continuous improvement and the values and principles nurtured and supported in the Toastmasters program.

Author's Preface

This speech was used in the Fall of 2005 to win the District 58 (South Carolina) Humorous Speech Contest. I had successfully competed through the Club, Area and Division contests, in every previous year I had participated in the Humorous contest. I just never had quite enough to actually win at the District level. I didn't even show up on the radar (1st, 2nd or 3rd) in any of those prior contests. I was nothing more than a not-very-funny footnote in the annals of District competition.

I can do humor. My talent lies more in situational – in the moment – humor. I found it quite another challenge to be funny, on purpose, for 5 to 7 minutes. Can you relate to that? Then I discovered that people laughed with me (or at me) more when I made fun of myself. It is called self-deprecating humor. Once I started to include this in my speeches, things changed.

This speech started out as a Club speech project "Show What You Mean" from the old Competent Toastmaster (CTM) basic manual It's original title was *"Lessons from the MotoCross of Life."* When I decided to compete again in 2005, one of my Club members reminded me that he thought that speech was one my funniest. I immediately resurrected it, dusted it off and took another look at what made it work and how to make it better

It's a very physical speech, as are many of my presentations. (I fall down twice during the delivery. Of course it is on purpose! I'm not a clumsy person!!) The humor comes as much from the presentation and timing as from the words. I try to help you "see" the speech, through the staging comments written beside the actual speech text. I hope it works for you. It is how I keep focused on all the components I feel are necessary to the successful delivery of any speech.

I changed the title to *"What Doesn't Kill Me"* (subtitled *"Makes Me Stronger"*), included audience participation in saying the key phrase, and was successful in Club, Area and Division contests. At the suggestion of my coaches, I changed the title to *"Hey! Watch This!"* and kept the audience participation for the District Contest. It was a very wise move.

The person mentioned by name in the speech (Jay Nodine, DTM PID from North Carolina) is a good friend, and very funny speaker, who was visiting for our Conference. He had been one of my humor coaches for this speech, and had given valuable advice the first year I competed in the International Speech Contest. I used him to anchor one of the the motorcycle incidents (you'll see which one), because most there knew him, thought he was funny and got a big kick out of hearing him included in the story.
It got a very big laugh!!

I was the last of five speakers and the audience began laughing when the title was given by the Contest Master, even before I had entered the room. I knew this was going to be a "Defining Moment!"

I hope you enjoy it!

May your words always touch Hearts and your Humor never fall flat!!

Douglas Wilson, DTM PDG
2nd Place Winner – 2006 World Championship of Public Speaking
Co-Author - "Win, Place & Show"
e-mail: dwwilsondtm@earthlink.net

"Hey! Watch This!"
by Douglas Wilson

Editor's Note: Douglas Wilson writes his speeches in a unique format to plan in detail his gestures, facial expressions, tone of voice, and movements on stage. We have endeavored to preserve his approach, in order to give our readers another tool in the art of speechwriting.

	Staging, gestures and notes
	/ = pause // = longer pause
	Center stage wearing black
What is it about a motorcycle	*three-piece suit topped with*
that makes grown men	*black Fedora -*
throw caution to the wind?	*Throw hat offstage like frisbee*
	exposing red-bandanna
Why is it -	*Take off suit jacket – put on*
when we climb aboard	*black motorcycle jacket*
one of those - bad boys	*Straddle imaginary motorcycle*
we become BAD BOYS?	*pull up jacket collar like the*
as Evel Knievel	*Fonz*
reincarnates in our bodies?	
And why is it the last words	*continue slightly crouched*
you will probably hear,	*straddle while gesturing to lips*

"Hey! Watch This!" by Douglas Wilson

from our *possessed* lips just before we do something truly Stu-pid is **"Hey!! Watch This!"** Will you say it with me? **"Hey! Watch this!"**	*left hand extended to crowd with waving motion towards self Invite audience to participate repeating wave of hand*
Mr Toastmaster, fellow toastmasters and anyone who has ever felt the wind in your hair // and bugs in your teeth	*gesture to TMOD(*) arms spread to include audience* *both hands slide around head pause - rub one finger over front teeth and grimace*
On the island of Guam I bought a shiny new Kawasaki motorcycle A big Bike!	*walk two paces stage right*
The next day I was riding back from the beach / on a slippery Coral road / up ahead I saw a man on a Honda // A Bigger Bike!!	*crouched straddle facing slightly right of front - left hand down to imaginary road right hand pointing ahead* *pause for effect here*
I was about to do something stupid and I said: **"Hey! Watch this!"**	*Look at audience with stupid grin and repeat inviting wave with left hand toward self inviting audience to join in.*
I zipped by him - so fast . . . Made his head spin. I looked back to see the look on his face and to see if he was impressed	*extra crouch with straddle to simulate speed & sound effects look back over left shoulder complete sentence looking at audience*

(*) TMOD stands for 'Toaastmaster of the day'

by Douglas Wilson — "Hey! Watch This!"

I hit a swarm of bugs

There were thousands of them
/ well /
There were hundreds of them
//
Ok - there was only one

But it was a BIG one
and it hit - SMACK -
in the middle of my goggles

Then the CORAL road
took a sharp turn to the left.

I was told
"You do NOT want to
get cut by Coral"

So I was v-e-r-y careful
not to fall down
on that coral road

So I didn't turn. //

That's right -
I went off that road -
into the ditch -
& into the trees

They were slapping me
in my face
At least it cleaned
the bug off my goggles!!

*turn head back to front and wave
left hand wildly in front of face –
warding off bugs
quick look at audience
pause
pleading look at audience
pause stand erect – lower head
and confess*

*show bug hit in middle of
goggles with right hand*

*show audience road turn with
left hand*

*stand and take step forward
out of story – explain to
audience*

*slight lower gesture to right
with right hand
step back into story – resume
straddle on cycle
pause*

*gesture to right then lower
hand to show ditch – turn
slightly left toward audience
and simulate with right hand
many tree branches hitting the
head and face*

*use left hand to wipe pretend
bug off goggles*

"Hey! Watch This!" by Douglas Wilson

One of the trees leaped at me- // It could happen!!	*two hands grab to left in surprise – pause – plead with audience*
It jerked me by my helmet off the motorcycle and slammed me on the ground. I went down faster than Hulk Hogan throwing Rick Flair in a body slam	*right hand becomes branch which slides up right side of face under helmet - stand erect and fall backward onto stage still on ground- feign rising and reach into back right pocket and*
I tried to get up but a man with a handkerchief slammed me down again to stop the bleeding	*pull out a red handkerchief and put on right forehead lie back down on left elbow with kerchief held to forehead*
Lucky Me!! / The guy I just passed // was a medical technician from the local hospital	*stand – dust off suit and jacket and step slightly forward to finish this narrative pause for audience response begin slow walk to stage-left*
I should have learned my lesson in High School	*gesturing with left hand to show regression of time*
My friend Robert showed me how to ride his new motorbike	*on left side of stage straddle a new bike facing directly into audience*
"Douglas you rev the engine with your right hand let go of the clutch with your left hand, and away she goes."	*turn right hand to speed up engine – extend fingers of left hand to show release and then extend left hand to show intended path of the bike - straddle crouch -*
COOL!! **"Hey! Watch This!"**	*big stupid grin at audience with inviting wave with left hand*

by Douglas Wilson   "Hey! Watch This!"   121

I revved that engine,	*right hand turns*
let go of that clutch,	*left hand extends*
and away she went	*left hand shows path forward*
and fell down	*Point to member of audience*
over by Jay Nodine //	*who happens to be a very funny person - pause*
Oh, It's ok. -	*stand and assure audience he's*
He wasn't hurt - //	*ok pause*
and neither was I / this time./	*pause again*
Maybe I'll get smarter	*walk a few paces stage-right*
when I get older	*showing passage of time again*
Years later in Texas	
I bought a Husqvarna Motocross	
racing bike,	
This was THE bike to have	
if you wanted to race MotoCross	
or ride cross country.	
	crouch on new bike and turn
It made a lot of noise-	*right hand making high pitched*
ying ying ying	*noise to simulate bike sound*
and had big knobby tires.	
I was trail riding -	*bike pointed to right of stage*
down in Mexico /	
- in a ditch -	*right hand extended forward*
beside the road. - //	*and down - sweep audience*
Oh it's ok	*with eyes with assuring look*
I meant to be in the ditch //	*sincere assurance – pause*
this time //	*another pause as head turns back to bike's path*
Up ahead I spied a Rock	*point at rock in path with left*
in the path.	*hand*
Can you tell me, why	*step out of story to discuss point*
no matter what road	*with audience –*

- or ditch we ride in life	*point to right at ditch*
there is always a rock in the middle of the road?	*point at imaginary rock*
	step back onto bike (straddle and
I kept telling myself	*crouch) pointing again at the rock*
"I'm NOT going to hit that rock." "I'm NOT going to hit that rock!" //	*slam right hand into left hand*
BAM - I hit that rock	*showing impact*
I did a swan dive	*body positioned for swan-dive*
that would have won	*arms extended – body straight*
a gold medal in the Olympics //	*and erect - pause*
if there had been a category for	*look at audience with look of*
"motorcycle ejects rider"	*dismay*
I landed on my head.	*gesture to head*
And guess where I landed?	*look at audience*
on the rock //	*point down to right*
No, not this rock	*point back down to left*
THAT rock //	*point again down to right*
There were only two rocks	*step out of story and explain the*
in that ditch all day - //	*dilemma – pause for*
and I hit both of them.	*response*
The bike was ok and so was I	*step back into story – dust off*
so we drove on down to	*clothing – pick up bike – straddle*
the roadside park where ALL the hot-shot bikers were	*and continue*
I'm going to show them	*stupid grin at the audience with*
what MY mean machine will do.	*slightly evil look on face*

(ying - ying - ying) That's right I was about to do / something stupid and I shouted - **"Hey!! - Watch This!!"** //	*rev engine with right hand* *another grin at the audience (they can probably see this coming) so gesture to invite them to join in*
I revved that engine, I popped that clutch and I did my *first* ever wheelie. // Oh! It was perfect!! ///	*turn right hand again extend fingers of left hand and extend arms straight forward still holding onto to handles voice pitch goes up excitedly as if achieving a dream!!*
I wish I had been on that bike!! // // but I couldn't let go- so at 30 miles an hour that bike plowed a 9" deep furrow in that dirt / that would have made a farmer proud. / dirt - spewing - all over me.	*Slight whimpering in voice big pause – big response slow jog to stage-right as if plowing a field with the bike* *show new trench with right hand extended down and moving forward frantic hand gestures showing dirt covering body*
When the bike went down, so did I. and everyone laughed // and everyone laughed!!!	*move hands down to left as bike falls then fall on the ground facing the audience stand and invite the audience to laugh with vigorous hand gestures*
Ladies and gentlemen I've learned some great lessons on this MotoCross called life.	*dust off the dirt walking back to center stage near front*

I've learned . . . /

When I'm lying in the ditch
wondering if my bike
is all banged up //
IT IS!!

I've learned,
when I'm zooming
down the road
at breakneck speed -
I probably want to lift my feet
up off the ground.

And some where - some time -
Be prepared to see something
really stu-pid - When you hear
"Hey!! Watch This!!"
// //
Mr Toastmaster

*point to location for first story
and speak with a slight moan -
remembering the event*

emphatically – voice pitch up

*turn slightly left – straddle and
crouch low*

lift left foot off the stage

*stand up and walk to edge of the
stage – speak in "Candid
Camera" style
gesture to invite audience to
participate in closing remark
pause
gesture in completion to TMOD*

Analysis

Douglas Wilson offers us another look at a textbook humorous speech successfully written and delivered for a Toastmaster audience. The heart of the speech, however, the concept of *"Hey! Watch This"*, is universal.

1. Costuming – Creating the Right Image
Douglas comes out in a 3-piece suit – expected attire for his contest – with a fedora covering up his costuming surprise, delivered with his first line. Throwing off the hat is symbolic of the audience throwing off their inhibitions, and preparing for a speech delivered by a dignified older man wearing a red bandanna! The humor is natural, and offered visually, as opposed to a written joke.

2. Catchy Cultural Reference – Reinforcing the Role
Two Evel Knievel references in one book (see Terry Canfield's *"Rules to Live By When Calling 911"*) proves that crazy stunts are fodder for funnyness anytime. In this case, the choice continues to craft an image in the listener's minds, as they project the Knievel image onto the speaker. Douglas again appeals to a middle age demographic with a Hulk Hogan/Rick Flair mention. If the reference is unknown, the term body-slam explains and reinforces the reference.

3. Sarcastic Set-Up
Douglas builds up his theme through sarcastic phrasing 'last words', 'possessed lips', 'truly stupid' – emphasized with a proper wise-acre tone. When the punch-line hits, we laugh at the sheer obviousness of it, and our own familiarity with using it at one point in our life (or many).

4. Physical Humor – A Clash of Images
Motorcycle adventures are ripe for gestures, and we see everything from crouching to hand-waving to insect splatters to

eventually falling to the ground. In addition to telling the story, humor is achieved at the site of watching an older man channel the stunts of his younger self. A caveat for potential tumblers – be cautious in how far you push your actions. If the audience is more concerned for your health that what you are saying, your connection will shatter.

5. Schadenfreude – With Hindsight
Schadenfreude is a term that denotes taking humor or enjoyment out of someone else's miseries. It is a driving force in our world, from slowing down traffic past an accident to creating action films such as *Die Hard*. In this case, we see our speaker is alive and healthy, offering up his motorcycling misfortunes for our entertainment. While races, spinouts, and crashes are deadly topics, we give ourselves permission to laugh, knowing, in this case at least, it all turns out okay.

6. The Topper – In Forward and Reverse
Topping is used several times for humorous effect: "big bike....BIGGER bike"; "Not this rock, THAT rock", "first-ever wheelie....wish I'd BEEN ON that bike". The reverse topper is also effective, as Douglas exaggerates his run in with a swarm of bugs – boldly going from thousands of bugs, to a more realistic portrayal of hundreds of bugs, to a final meek admission of one bug – then grabbing the moment to shift forward again "But it was a BIG one!". In these moments we begin to empathize with the speaker as he 'reveals the truth', and allow ourselves to again be swept away with the final punch-line.

7. Props – Leveraging Your Audience
In this instance, Douglas knew his friend, Jay Nodine, would be in the audience, and would be known by others in attendance. A references to him in the story builds credibility, and assigns positive attention to the audience, allowing them to become part of the story. The funnier Jay is viewed by the audience, the funnier the reference becomes. Researching your audiences in a

corporate setting can provide you with similar openings, even if they are for exaggeration vs. factual recounting. Referencing a company celebrity (CEO, manager, employee of the year, or otherwise well-known personality) can build your rapport with the audience, when with the right intention. Before taking this approach – do your research, and meet them ahead of time if possible, to avoid any awkward results.

8. Callbacks – Comedy in Cue

The phrase "Hey! Watch this!" becomes an instant signal for humor to come. By repeating it at key moments in the speech, the story moves along, and keeps a rhythm designed to keep the audience engaged. It also creates a 'catch-phrase' the audience will remember and use afterwards. You know you've been effective as a speaker when folks later in the day are shouting to each other "Hey! Watch this" as they pull the tablecloth out from under a full table setting.

By simply taking out the Toastmaster references, the stories in this speech stand strong. At one point, a motivational message is touched upon, when he questions why, no matter what road we go down, there are rocks in our path. While these may appear to be stories swapped at a compfire, they can be applied in many ways. Picture it as a moralilty tale at a safety conference – creating an uplifting mood for the crowd while still giving them a takeaway phrase to anchor the concepts to.

Stories of our own misfortunes are effective both as inspiration and humor. The connection built with the audience by revealing even the silliest of life's adventures will leave them ready and willing to hear what you have to teach them by speech end.

Susan Lamb

Susan has been called an inspiring and dynamic speaker by her peers and past clients.

She comes to the lectern with a winning combination of passion and humour. Her sincerity and honesty have been deemed her most captivating qualities.

In a ten year period during her thirties, Susan lost her house, her business, her sister, her father, she had a miscarriage, her mom almost died from a brain aneurism, her youngest child was diagnosed with a form of autism, and she almost lost her someone she loved to depression.

Although she was financially and emotionally bankrupt at times, Susan chose to let these heartaches hold her up instead of drag her down. She shares with audiences how to search through the rubble of despair and find hope and happiness.

In her presentation called "Where do you Live?" She illustrates how many of us spend most of our lives living in the land of "Make Believe" or the land of "Use to Be" when we really need to live in the land of "I am" where we embrace all that we are and stop worrying about all that we are not.

Susan also teaches public speaking to others and is currently teaching a continuing education course for the Dufferin Peel Catholic School

Board called "Speaking for Success" and another called "Communication Secrets of Success".

Susan has also won several high profile public speaking contests throughout her career; most recently she advanced all the way to the 2008 Toastmasters District 60 International Speech Contest where she placed third out of 1200 speakers.

Contact her at:
Susan Lamb-Robinson
572 Lynd Avenue, Mississauga, Ontario L5G 2M2
Cell Phone: 416-677-3554
Home Phone: 905-278-3671
Email: susanlamb12@rogers.com

Author's Preface

I wrote this speech to pay homage to my wonderful KIDS and to get back at them for all the crazy things they have put my husband and I through.

When we get together these are all the stories we tease each other about and the ones that will go down in our family's Story Hall of Fame.

So I sat down and wrote them all out in point form and then decided which ones might play for the biggest laughs. Then I tried to bring each one to life by adding dialogue and characters wherever I could. Then I thought of the theme to weave them all together (the acronym) and that's when my *KIDS* came alive.

Believe it or not, all the stories in the speech are true, except that I may have exaggerated a bit, or altered the timing of something for effect, or added one more element to make it more outrageous.

Also, in one case, I attributed the actions of one child for another so that each KID got equal time in the speech. Can I help it that one of my 4 kids never gets into to trouble! (He just turned 15 and now he's working on it!)

Anyway, after I won my club contest with my first version, I set out to speak in front of a lot of different audiences to see if the material held up. I spoke in front of a group of teachers, a group of engineers (now there's a fun crowd!) and even a group of nuclear scientists. The good news was, didn't matter what the audience members did for a living they could all relate because most had children, or at least nieces and nephews, and knew exactly what I was talking about.

My biggest obstacle actually became my delivery, since much of the speech relies on timing and pacing. Sometimes I had to deadpan a line and other times I had to let it reek of sarcasm.

In particular though, I had a problem pausing long enough during the laughter. Yes I'll admit it here – I was afraid of the pause.

But you see it was my first speech contest, and by the time I made it to District (top 10 out of 1200) I was petrified. I know I rushed through and as one of the World Champions of Public Speaking said (Not sure which one) – I treaded on the audiences laughter – but at least they laughed.

I should also share with you that when I first had this idea – I thought "I can't do it – my KIDS would kill me if they ever find out I am doing a speech about them". Then I thought – "Hey they'll never hear it so I'm safe. So I went ahead and took the plunge".

Problem was, my children did find out and believe me, they weren't laughing.

One day when I was at work my oldest daughter was using my computer and found my tape recorder that I was using to practice my speech on and listened to it. When I got home that night – I was greeted by an angry mob who wanted more than my croissants -- they wanted my blood!

Luckily I thought quickly and was able to appeal to their vanity and told them how famous they were becoming out there as I won each subsequent level of the contest. They eventually settled down and a couple of them were even perversely proud.

When they heard that I would be competing at the top level of the contest – the District 60 Humorous Speech Contest – they all offered to run out and do some more horrifying things so I had even better material!

I, of course, declined that generous offer and went on to the District contest. Although I did not place in the top three, it was still an amazing experience, as I received so many wonderful comments.

In fact, one lady pulled me aside later in the conference and shared with me that her teenage son had just come home that past weekend from University and informed her that he had gotten his girlfriend pregnant and would have to drop out. She told me that she was so angry and devastated by the news that she kicked him out of the house.

She told me, however, after hearing my speech that she rushed right out and called her son and told him to come back home and that they would work it all out -- together.

I asked her what it could possibly have been in what was supposed to be a humorous speech that changed her mind about such a serious thing. She put her hand on my shoulder and said "If you're still able to laugh about all this and find the lighthearted side of it– then so can I. You convinced me that no matter what – it was all going to work out and someday we'd be able to look back and laugh."

Wow – who knew shilling for laughs at the expense of my kids would actually help someone. Needless to say, hearing her words was better than any trophy I could have ever received!

"KIDS" *by Susan Lamb*

Good evening ladies and gentlemen.

I stand before you today as the mother of 4 children -- 4 wonderful children who range in age from 11 to 21.

My 2 girls I adopted when they were just 1 and 3 -- and I have been their mom for eighteen years.

My 2 boys however I birthed the hard way -- with a lot of screaming and tears -- and that was just by my husband!

Now I love these 4 kids with all my heart -- but -- like any one with children will tell you -- **KIDS** -- is really just an acronym for -- **Kept In Debt and Shock!**

It's true!

As long as you have KIDS you will be Kept In Debt and Shock!

I know what some of you are thinking. You hate it when other people refer to their children as KIDS -- after all they're not baby goats!

Well let me tell you something! -- if you met my kids -- you'd probably think they were a bunch of animals!

Take grocery day for instance -- At my house it's more like the running of the bulls.

I come in through the front door with the Foodmart bags and it's like I'm waving a red flag.

Out of no where come 4 rampaging children stampeding from all parts of the house trying to corner me in the kitchen.

Suddenly I feel like a cop trying to prevent a robbery.

"Back away from the croissants!"

"Put the pepperoni stick down!"

"You have the right to remain silent, once you finish eating those chips!"

And you want to know something else that's shocking? -- how much it costs to feed 4 KIDS!

All my children may be tall and thin-- but they eat like longshoremen!

Now a couple of them swear like sailors too and that's where more of the shock comes in.

And what about the cost for home repairs!?

I'm the only one I know that gets a personalized Christmas Card from the manager of Home Depot.

Oh and the property damage – it's not just limited to our house!

Oh no -- when Conner was 4, in one week he flooded the babysitter's upstairs bathroom and drove my van into her garage door!

Child care expenses for the week $2500 -- shocked look on my husbands face - priceless.

You know it's been seven years since that happened and the babysitter's husband still grits his teeth when we pass his house!

And I can't even go to the neighborhood barbershop anymore – not since Riley blurted out one day while we were waiting for a hair cut – "Hey Mommy, why is that man only getting his hair cut in the middle of his head?"

The man of course was going bald and based on the look he shot me -- he didn't need my kid reminding him of that.

And another time, Conner told his teacher that his grandmother was into Healthcare Prostitution – I was horrified and corrected him, "Conner your grandmother's in a Health Care INSTITUTION!!"

Can I share a secret with you? If I'm really honest -- I think my neighbors think my family's crazy!

You see a couple of years ago, when my oldest daughter Tara broke up with her boyfriend, he came over to our house at 3 in the morning, climbed up on our garage roof, balling his eyes out, trying to tap on her window with a hockey stick begging her to please come out and talk to him.

I had to get up outta bed, go downstairs and out into our driveway in my pajamas and try and talk this crying boyfriend off the roof!

---before my husband came out and gave him something to cry about!

I also had to apologize to our elderly neighbour Mrs Ardezzi across street, who came out with her lawn hose when she heard all the racket thinking the boyfriends crying was a stray cat in heat.

I told her several times how sorry I was for all the commotion with the boyfriend. She told me not to worry about it, because apparently when he wasn't on the garage roof, my daughter was sneaking him in through our back door.

And speaking of boyfriends -- both my daughter's taste in this area has been well -- questionable and yes -- sometimes even shocking.

We had this one guy that looked like he was in a boy band and had sunglasses surgically adhered to his face.

Another guy that looked so scary he looked like he belonged in prison -- which by the way is where he eventually ended up!

And another one that looked like he'd been doing way too many drugs.

Well -- that's what I thought when I first met him.

Because you see it was Christmas time and he was sitting on the couch looking at all the pretty Christmas lights on our tree with a really stunned look on his face.

I said to my youngest daughter Kaylha when he left, "I don't appreciate him coming around here when he's high!"

She screamed at me totally outraged, "Mom, Johnny doesn't even do drugs!"

I feel kind of bad -- cause I was actually disappointed when she said that – because that just meant he was stupid!

In closing, my husband and I experienced what I suppose is considered the biggest shock a parent can go through

-- when our then nineteen year old daughter came home and told us

....she was pregnant.

We eventually realized it wasn't the end of the world -- especially since the father of the baby wasn't the guy from prison!

So now not only do we have four KIDS but we have a beautiful baby grandkid.

---and although it's true that I continue to believe that KIDS is still an acronym for Kept In Debt & Shock

I would be remiss if I didn't tell those that were considering having children that it also sometimes means **Kept In Delight & Smiles** too

– just not as often!

Analysis

There is no more universal source for humor in a speech than children. Even if your listeners have none, they at one time were one! In *"KIDS"*, Susan Lamb offers up a treasure trove of tattle tales on her own children, weaving them into and around an overall point of keeping a positive attitude regardless of what your children do, through the very humorous devices she's showcasing.

1. Humorous Open – Permission to Laugh
While the beginning of the speech starts in autobiographical fashion, Susan quickly puts her audience at ease with a quick, if familiar, turn of circumstances as she describes her two boys being birthed through screaming. Her husband's screaming, that is.

2. Alphabet Soup – Making Mirth Memorable
Turning KIDS into Kept In Debt & Shock creates a quick pneumonic for the audience while creating humor everytime the term is repeated thereafter. While she shifts the acronym in the end (Kept In Delight & Smiles), it still reminds us of the first usage, even while creating a defining point in the speech. Acronyms are common in speaking, often turning an audience against the speaker if they're staid and predictable. Using them as points of humor gives the audience a reason to keep up with you, and builds your credibility as a speaker.

3. Dialogue as Storyteller
Susan slips into storyteller mode easily, grabbing dialogue from her everday life and exaggerating them for humor's sake. "Back away from the croissants, put the pepperoni sticks down, you have the right to remain silent, once you finish those chips" are believeable quotes from the speaker who is laying her foundation as an easygoing, pun-loving individual.

Later in the speech – she brings humor out from the dialogue of her children. Only from children will lines such as "why is that man only getting his hair cut in the middle of his head" and "grandmother's into healthcare prostitution" elicit a simultaneous mix of shock, empathy, appreciation, and belly-laughter.

4. Humorous Imagery
The speech often compares its subjects (children) with other examples: baby goats, bulls, longshoremen, and sailors. Each case draws a picture in the minds of the audience, and are clear enough to help keep the audience up with the pace of the speech.

5. Sarcasm – Teenagers Make Cynics of Us All
Susan drips with sarcasm discussing her daughters' choices of boyfriends, to the point of saying she's disappointed to realize one is stupid as opposed to stoned, and finding gratitude in the thought that her daughter comes home from college pregnant, but NOT from the boyfriend who ended up in prison. Only a mother can poke fun at her own children with such precision, creating an atmosphere where the audience feels comfortable laughing along with her.

The speech presented here is short by design, and sacrifices some cohesiveness and the opportunity to delve in-depth into its theme in the process. While the main point is anchored in the acronym to close the speech, the speech shows potential for easy expansion to a 25-45 minute speech, simply by fleshing out the material with additional details, shifting the pace from rapid-fire humor to humorous storytelling, and making the life-changing point crystal-clear to her audience.

KIDS effectively uses humor to keep the audience both interested in the speech and secure in the knowledge that all works out in the end. While the subject matter is emotionally charged, Susan controls the message with her pacing, tone of voice, and positive bent.

Michael Davis

Helping YOU live your passion...this is what drives Michael Davis. As a professional speaker, Michael's focus is to help others in two areas: creating financial security and peace of mind, and, becoming the best possible speaker and presenter you can be. He believes that when you eliminate financial worries and stress, you free your mind to pursue your deepest desires and dreams. Once you have this clarity of purpose, you then need to be able to tell the world.

A professional speaker since 1998, Michael is a keynote speaker and also mentors speakers in the process of creating memorable messages and delivering them in a dynamic, memorable style. Michael's experience as a two-time semi-finalist in Toastmasters International speech competition, as well as winning two District evaluation championships, gives him unique qualifications to help you improve your speaking and presentation skills. His past clients have included General Electric, Johnson & Johnson, and Great American Insurance.

As a financial advisor, Michael teaches a unique approach to wealth creations, protection, and retention. He shows how to create financial plans which overcome the four biggest obstacles to financial success; how to efficiently protect your family and your money from the unexpected; and how to create and leave a significant legacy for your family. Michael's strategies have helped families create plans which provide long-term security and financial freedom.

Michael lives in Fairfield, Ohio with his family. He enjoys teaching and mentoring, listening to his extensive music and comedy collection, participating in sports, and reading.

Michael is the author of the audio CDs "Evaluate to Elevate" and "It's Called Long-Term Care PLANNING". If you'd like to contact Michael about presenting at your event, call 513.619.2564, email him at SpeakingCPR@live.com, or visit his website, www.SpeakingCPR.com.

Author's Preface

"Question Man" was a speech literally written over breakfast with Chris Nachtrab, a fellow Toastmaster. I explained to him a survey I had just completed with my financial clients. The survey revealed that my clients felt my best attribute as an advisor was my ability and willingness to listen.

That information sparked an idea…a superhero who went around listening to people who felt neglected. As a contrast, Chris suggested an "anti-hero", the stereotypical male who isn't a good listener. From that conversation, the framework of the speech was created. A conversation between my wife Gerri and me served as the central story to the speech.

Originally, *"Question Man"* was created for Toastmasters International speech competition. From the first presentation, I loved this speech. It was fun to write and present, and continually improve. The humor is rooted in its visual aspects, which are noted in the text. It has been said that to win speech contests, you need to do something different. The 'costuming' of this speech was definitely different!

There were dozens of revisions to the speech, with the most drastic coming after each of the 23 live practices before Toastmasters audiences. Aside from the concept of the superhero and anti-hero, and the central story with my wife Gerri, the final version of *"Question Man"* is dramatically different from the original version.

Each time I presented the speech, one idea consistently came up in my evaluations… "You should wear a shirt with a Big "S" on your chest for the anti-hero". As World Champion speaker Darren LaCroix has said, if you keep hearing the same idea over and over from many people, you have an opportunity for humor. So…the costumed hero and anti-hero were born!

Without a doubt, the added clothing twist made the speech memorable, and provided the most humor. The other source of humor was the conversation between my wife and me. Writing this speech reminded me that the best humor is not forced, and does not come from one-liner jokes. The speech challenged me to be more physical, and the humor flowed from real-life, not made up jokes or stories.

Based on audience reactions, this speech has been and continues to be a hit. It has become a 'signature story'. In the aftermath of my contest success, I have created a listening workshop centered around the story. If you'd like more details about the workshop, feel free to contact me at SpeakingCPR@live.com or [513] 619.2564.

Question Man

by Michael Davis

If you had been sitting with my Gerri and me on our old tan couch, you would have felt her frustration. She was **trying** to tell me about our sons, Sean and Brenden, while I read the newspaper, oblivious to her feelings. *"Mike, I'm so frustrated with the boys; all they do is argue and talk back to me!"* Never taking my eyes off the paper, I grunted, *"Uh huh"*. She continued, *"Every day is one big fight to get them to do their homework and their chores!"* Again, with a little more boredom thrown in, I mumbled, *"Okay."* *"Michael, if they don't stop..... I'm gonna kill 'em!"* Slightly lowering the newspaper and glancing over the top, I replied *"Go ahead..."* Frustration turned to ANGER! Gerri knew the only sound I was hearing was *"wah wah wah"*. How would YOU have felt?

Fortunately, the boys and I are still alive today. But that conversation between my wife and I underscores a big problem today - many people are very poor listeners. Our world is so full of noise - ringing cell phones, kids playing video games all day, 24-hour cable TV - sometimes doesn't feel impossible to just...STOP...and give someone your undivided attention? If **you** are frequently hearing *"wah wah wah"* when others speak, you are hurting your relationships.

I know because for much of my life, I was a terrible listener. Whenever **any**body tried to have a heart-to-heart talk with me, I didn't hear that person. Actually, I took on a whole new persona. I became (rip off tie and rip open shirt to expose a t-shirt with a giant Superman 'S' on the front)... **Solution Man! The problem solving Super Hero.** Faster than a speeding bullet!! More powerful than a locomotive!! Unable to <u>hear</u> a <u>single word you say</u>!! He's so self-absorbed, all he wants to so is quickly solve your problem so he can get back to his daily routine.

Is there a Solution Man in your life? Is it possible *you* are a Solution Man...or woman! Solution Man's BIGGEST problem is that he doesn't make an emotional connection with any one, although he thinks he does. At the end of our couch talk, Gerri said *"Mike, you're not listening to me!"* In my head, I heard Solution Man, *"Of course I'm listening, I'm going to solve your problem, good citizen."* Disgustedly, she said, *"You don't really hear anybody...you just don't get it!"*

That stung like a swarm of hornets. After a couple of days of serious soul searching, I realized she was right. I didn't 'get it,' I wasn't hearing the people in my life. I finally understood that my poor listening was hurting the people I love. That was painful. After some time, that pain motivated me to improve my world, to find a better way to listen. I read books, listened to CDs and tapes, then, I found an answer... an article written by Dr Tony Allesandra, a communications expert. He wrote that one key to effective listening is asking open ended questions, questions that can't just be answered with a 'yes' or 'no' answer; questions like *"how can I help you"* or *"how is this affecting you"*.

Those questions encourage the other person to open up, speak from the heart. They also let that person know that you **really... do... care.** When someone feels that you care and that you're really listening, you make a heart-to-heart connection.

This insight inspired me; I wanted to rush out and improve my relationships. But first, I had to shed the shackles of Solution Man. I became...(rip open shirt to expose a t-shirt with a giant '?' on the front)...... **Question Man!**

Two weeks later, Gerri and I were back on that same tan couch. *"Mike, the boys have been arguing with me a lot, and I don't know what to do".* In my head, I heard Solution Man struggling to speak up, but Question Man quickly took over. *"Honey, what's that doing to you when they act like that?"* Slightly startled, she started to tell me. When she saw that I was paying attention, she opened up, poured out her heart. After a-b-o-u-t.... 25 minutes... she said, *"You know, what really bothers me isn't the talking back or the attitude, it's that I don't feel any love or respect from the boys. That's what hurts".* Aha!! She felt comfortable saying that to me because she knew I was listening, and not trying to fix the problem.

Then she said, *"What do you think?"......* Oh NO! Not **that** question! Again, Solution Man tried to rear his ugly head.... but, Question Man again jumped in. *"Gerri, I don't have an opinion or a solution, I just wanted to understand how you feel."......*

When she came to...... OK!! She didn't *really pass* out... but she sure looked like she was going to. What she did was throw her arms around me, and squeezed me with a huge hug. We felt closer than we had in six months. That experience taught me that... **the shortest distance between two hearts is... through your ears.**

Listening isn't easy. I still have my Solution Man days. You **can** become a **better** listener if you'll adopt Question Man's philosophy of asking enough open-ended questions and really listening to the answers until you can say "I understand. I get it."

Fellow citizens of Toastopolis, I leave you with these questions... "Is there someone in your life who needs you to listen, right now? Which questions do you need to ask that person? How will that relationship change when you listen to what that person is really saying?

Now, get out there! Ask those questions. And listen. After all, the fastest way to connect two hearts is... **through your** (gesture to audience to encourage them to say) **ears**.

Analysis

"Question Man" is not a humorous speech, by nature. It is a fine example of an informative speech using humor to keep the audience interested. Take the humor out of this speech, and it becomes textbook classroom teacher material. With the humor component? It becomes entertaining, unusual, and most importantly, *memorable*.

1. Humorous Opening
While the build-up takes about 25 seconds of narrative combined with dialogue, the element of surprise creates a payoff in the familiarity of 'wah-wah-wah', connecting with most any audience member. In addition, by not going too far over the top in his open, Michael sets the stage for his next major use of humor.

2. Costuming – Popping Buttons
The ripping open of one's shirt to reveal a super-hero costume is a classic tool of speakers everywhere. When its done by someone in the middle of a relatively serious speech, the shock itself creates laughter from those caught off guard. Topping it later in the speech with a second costume reveal creates an anything goes atmosphere, that gives the audience complete permission to giggle and guffaw, while continuing to move the speech forward without distracting from the main point.

3. Rule of Three – Humor and Impact
Keeping momentum from the costume reveal, Michael goes down a familiar path with a twist. 'faster than a speeding bullet, more powerful than a locomotive, but he doesn't hear a single word you have to say'. Moments later, he uses another version of the Rule of Three as he makes a point about listening, using pauses as he emphasizes 'really...do...care'. The payoff word hits its mark. He uses it again in addressing the audience with questions as he moves to his close.

4. Voice Characterization – Heroic Intonations

We can hear the speakers voice deepen each time he reveals a super-hero persona, and speaks within the character – even as he encourages the 'citizens of Toastopolis (a funny twist on his audience, a group of Toastmasters)' with serious rhetorical questions. Now picture the same dialogue without the change in voice. The humor is deadened, the audience loses a cue to laugh, and lessens the impact of the Costuming. When a speaker chooses to get to the end of the high dive platform, not taking the dive makes the preceding effort a worthless exercise.

5. Self as Punchline – The Humble Student

Michael sets himself up as the fall guy, taking the hit for the audience. By relearning his own lesson, he takes the place of his audience, allowing people to laugh at HIM instead of focusing on their own miscommunications. To clearly knock his audience off their center, he turns part clown by way of the costume changes, all in pursuit of making his point clear and memorable.

6. Callback Close – Laugh to Learn

For much of the last third of *'Question Man'*, Michael moves into teacher/trainer mode, demonstrating technique to the audience. By reintroducing the super-hero theme, and then the voice characterization, he reminds the audience of how much fun the speech was, milks a final laugh, and then lowers the boom on a final emotional point for them to take home.

The concept and format of *'Question Man'* can crossover into many fields, from sales to management to human resources to parenting. I would say Michael can take his super-hero persona in front of virtually any audience without being seen as over the top, with two caveats: venue and familiarity.

The bigger the venue, the better for this type of costuming technique. A small conference room may be overwhelmed by this level of showmanship. Your familiarity with the audience is essential in all speaking situations, but especially when taking your speech to extremes. Do your research. Call the meeting planner and find out what the culture of your audience will be. What mood will they be in? What is the occasion surrounding your event? You don't have to reveal what you are doing to the meeting planner, but you must be willing to accept the risks inherent in surprising those who hire you.

The speech serves as a terrific example of using humor as spice instead of steak. The speech is clearly intended to teach, with humor helping the message be more palatable. The audience laughs, and the audience learns. When it comes time to use the information, the laughter remembered will bring it to the forefront faster than any of the dry, barren lectures so often found in the world of teaching and training today.

Punchlines

Eleven speeches, over thirty humor tools. A good start. Since this book is called a 'Guide' and not an 'Encyclopedia', don't be surprised if you notice new and different ways of using humor now that you've sharpened your skills. Below is a complete listing of the methods of humor discussed, with a brief description, for your reference.

Exaggerating the Familiar – creating a bigger view of a commonly perceived situation
Using Self as Punchline – using yourself as the butt of jokes, including hypothetical situations
Dialog as Storyteller – describing humorous events as an outside observer
Rule of Three – it starts okay, then gets bigger, then twists faster than an elected politician
Catchy Cultural References – comparisons to well known celebrities or newsworthy situations
Position Switch – putting yourself in the place of another character to create absurdity
Stage Persona – turning yourself into someone else for the entirety of a speech
Innuendos – typically veiled sexual humor, though racial and political can seep in as well
Gestures – sudden, exaggerated movements to illustrate the punchline
The Recognized – referring to commonly known events and adding a humorous twist
Callbacks – referring back to prior humor, or failed humor
Props – any foreign object on stage used to punctuate or create humor
Physical Humor – classic pratfalls and self-injury
Voice of the Audience – creating humor from your audience by voicing what they may be thinking

Wordplay – putting words or phrases together that normally don't
Humorous Open – using humor immediately to signal your audience to go ahead and laugh
Creating Villains – giving the audience someone to hate, and enjoy humor at the sake of
Voice characterizations – it looks like you, but it sure doesn't sound like you!
Costuming – wearing something extraordinary to back-up the humor in your speech
Creating a Character – the funny relative, employer, et al
The Unexpected – a surprise twist that shocks the audience to the point of laughter
Alphabet Soup – funny acronyms with funny meanings
Self-Deprecating Opening – making your imperfections the object of humor
Sarcasm – revealing and edgy double-edged commentary
Humorous Imagery – don't just hear the whoopee cushion, see its rubbery brilliance
Silly Singing – made up songs, or oddly sung lyrics to support the message
Sound Effects – yes, it's when you say "Vroom Vroom" on stage
Edginess – pushing levels of taste with sexual, political, or racial humor
Tailored Humor – humor developed after researching the audience
Sarcastic Set-Up – serious sounding statements that take on an attitude; sarcastic misdirection
Schadenfruede – humor based on another's misfortune
The Topper – a final reference or statement that adds humor to a list of references or statements

Go Ahead and Laugh is meant to inspire as well as instruct, and while reading you've probably come up with several ideas of your own for stories and humor. Start a humor log – a notebook you carry around, a folder on your computer to store ideas that come to you. Consider purchasing a digital audio recorder, which you can speak into whenever inspiration strikes. Humor happens all around you everyday. Train yourself to watch for it, and then record it for future story material.

Finally, remember humor for humor's sake works only in specific settings. In the vast majority of settings, always hold your humor up to a standard of "does this humor support and drive forward my message?" An occasional throwaway line is fine, but proceed with caution. Today's audiences are more likely than ever to take an off-the-cuff, unrelated line, down there own internal thought processes, and getting them to reconnect is a challenge you don't want to face.

The next time you find yourself in front of an audience, we hope you give these ideas a try. And, most likely, your audience is hoping you do as well. Go have fun with your audiences, and tell them... Go Ahead and Laugh!

Resources

From the Authors

www.SpeakWithHumor.com (Additional Humor Resources)
www.RichHopkins.com
www.DanWeedin.com
www.PalmoCarpino.com
www.SNPresentations.com (Sarfaraz Nazir)
www.RussDantu.com
www.StrategiesForWomensGrowth.com (Kay Fittes)
www.LearningWithLaughter.com (Charlie Wilson)
www.CarrieWarren.com
www.TCanfield.com (Terry Canfield)
www.SpeakingCPR.com (Michael Davis)
www.dwwilsondtm@earthlink.net (Douglas Wilson)
www.susanlamb12@rogers.com (Susan Lamb)

Others mentioned in the book:

www.DarrenLaCroix.com
www.JudyCarter.com
www.PatriciaFripp.com
www.CraigValentine.com
www.DavidBrookTexas.com
www.JimKey.com
www.WorldChampionsEdgeNet.com

For Information on Foreign Cultures

www.culturegrams.com

Made in the USA
Charleston, SC
10 April 2012